HELL'S PRISONER

HELL'S PRISONER

The Shocking True Story of an
Innocent Man Jailed for over Eleven Years
in Indonesia's Most Notorious Prisons

CHRISTOPHER V.V. PARNELL

MAINSTREAM
PUBLISHING

EDINBURGH AND LONDON

The names of various individuals have been changed.

First published in Great Britain in 2003 by
MAINSTREAM PUBLISHING COMPANY (EDINBURGH) LTD
7 Albany Street
Edinburgh EH1 3UG

Reprinted 2006

First published under the title *The Sunday Smuggler*
in Australia in 2002 by HarperCollins Publishers

ISBN 1 84018 704 2

A catalogue record for this book is available from the British Library

Typeset in Distress, Gill & Stone
Printed and bound in Great Britain by William Clowes Ltd, Beccles, Suffolk

I dedicate this book
to the victims of life:

The Spaniard – Antonio Vidderetta
The Chook – James Cook
My Daughter (Tina) – Christina Teresa Parnell
And the many others; now all dead.

Until the chains are never more
Will they place their feet on Paradise's shore
When chains are gone for ever more.

Take me, take me, take me,
To that place of peace
Ease me of my sorrows
I ask you, Lord, please, please.
The shadows gather around me
I walk a long dark passage here
My heart's so full of fear, of fear.
Build me, build me, build me,
Give me strength so I can be
Away from all this anguish
Free. . . Free. . . Free

Words taken from the walls of a death row cell
on Madura Island, Indonesia.

Author Unknown

Translated by
Christopher V. V. Parnell, 1989

CONTENTS

Author's Note		9
Prologue	Malang, Shitsville, Indonesia, 1992	13
Chapter 1	Bleeding Walls	15
Chapter 2	Hello – Is There Anybody out There?	25
Chapter 3	The Demon Shows its Face	41
Chapter 4	The Judge Had a Bad Breakfast . . .	55
Chapter 5	The Secret Ladder	61
Chapter 6	The Graduates of Murphy's Law	83
Chapter 7	Shadow People	93
Chapter 8	Goodbye, Custard Apples	107
Chapter 9	The Vomit Comet	121
Chapter 10	For the Cost of a Watch	143
Chapter 11	Shake Me, Wake Me When it's Over	157
Chapter 12	Riot to Make it Right	177
Chapter 13	And the Angels Wept	197
Chapter 14	'Saul, Saul, Saul'	207
Epilogue	When Nightmares End	215
Acknowledgements		221

AUTHOR'S NOTE

This book, *Hell's Prisoner*, truly did start from humble beginnings . . . at first I was going to write a letter, which somehow never got posted. That letter grew with other unposted letters and thoughts I'd scribbled down on scraps of paper to become a kind of *Diary of the Damned*. From those scraps of paper scrawled and scribbled upon well over ten years ago I have created this book. A book, I hope, that will not only be chewing gum for the eyes, but something that will leave a lasting impression upon you, the reader.

All in all, I was incarcerated for eleven years, one month, three weeks, five days, and, well bugger it, eleven hours. I stopped counting the minutes and seconds after the first ten years.

During these eleven years, I served time in five of Indonesia's prisons, which made me somewhat of a tourist in their prison system, a novelty no less . . . and . . . a novelty no more.

I managed to smuggle out of the prison most of my papers, letters, memoirs from my diaries, page by page. This feat took many, many years.

Pens, papers, books and literature of all sorts were all treasured possessions that I jealously guarded. They were all hard to come by but with a great deal of luck, a small fortune in bribes and slings and the occasional dose of brown nosing, and, most importantly, the help of my many loyal Christian friends, I managed to score enough paper to keep a record of prison life, which was no small feat. To get my writing paper, I would pilfer, pillage, steal or liberate whatever I could, whenever I could. If I could steal it from the administration office, the storeroom, the kitchen, or the visiting rooms, I would. It was all fair game as long as I wasn't caught! The prison offices were closed on Sundays and this gave me the opportunity to wander through and grab some paper. But not so much as to get caught, just a couple of sheets at a time. Sundays were the days when I committed 90 per cent of my illicit deeds: smuggling mail, medicine, or money in or out.

In total I spent four of these eleven years of prison life in solitary confinement; some cells were less than 2 metres by 2 metres. Sometimes I was in a darkened cell so pitch black that the silence screamed; it was a darkness where I could not see my hand, although it was only inches from my face.

I was in a place where time knows no boundaries and where the loneliness is an empty abyss, where for months my only mode of distraction or entertainment was a single button.

I flicked this button against an unseen wall and then I would spend hours in this black void searching for it . . . my button! I would search for it on my hands and knees, crawling and scratching, picking and feeling in a desperate search to locate the button.

How long would it take me to find it? Testing myself, using my ears to listen to the tinkle, tic tic of a button, as it was flicked up against the wall, then bouncing and rolling around a black dirt-encrusted floor.

Where did it land?

Imagine where it landed. I did . . . eventually. Nine times out of ten, I could reach over and pick up the button in the exact position that it came to rest, without turning my head or using my eyes, for they were useless in the darkness of my cell.

While locked away for those 11 long years, I did a lot of soul searching. I guess I was given an opportunity that few other people have. I discovered myself. I discovered how hungry a man can be. I discovered how much pain a man can take before his mind deserts him, and I discovered the cold dark depths of loneliness and isolation.

These alone are all great discoveries, yet they were not the greatest.

During these years, I discovered strength in myself that I never knew existed before.

A strength of compassion. A strength of understanding. A strength in the faith and belief that all those heartbreaking, soul scarring, evil times would one day end.

Being a foreign prisoner in Indonesia, during President Soeharto's reign of power, and an Australian prisoner at that, meant my future was never certain.

From one day to another I never was sure if I would eat . . . or even live to see another day.

Sometimes my very survival depended on how the Australian government and the Indonesian government were getting on.

I had left Australia at the age of 19. During the late 1970s and into the early 1980s, I owned a number of buses that travelled from Kathmandu to Varanasi, Benares, Agra, New Delhi, Bombay and Goa.

My bus services were more regular than the local lines, though in some circles they wore the tarnished brand of 'Freak Buses'. I had buses running from New Delhi to Karachi, Lahore, Islamabad, through the Khyber Pass and onto Kabul.

In Afghanistan my buses were well known and when travelling through the northern frontier providences, Pakistani government officials would often travel with me for safety.

My wife and children lived happily with me in Kathmandu, living the only life that they had known. And I living the only life that I had known.

I had been the proprietor and owner of the Kathmandu Riding Academy, rubbing shoulders with royalty and riff raff, diplomats, dignitaries and degenerates.

Servants, status, cars and cash at the age of 32 – I had been living a boy's own adventure, a little Biggles to the max.

Until one day, life, destiny, fate or Karma – call it what you like – stepped in and changed my world completely.

Once I was the master of 30 servants, with a legion of friends and helpers at my disposal.

But now it would seem that . . . yesterday's king is today's goat!

I stopped and looked around me . . . I was in a prison cell in Indonesia. Framed for a crime that I had not committed, asking myself, while scratching my head. 'How did you get yourself into all this shit, Ollie?'

So the story begins . . .

MALANG, SHITSVILLE, INDONESIA, 1992

A story of truth or a story of fiction?
Take it as you will . . .

Here I sit, nearly 40 years of age, with the knowledge that my eyes and my strength are starting to fail me. I have already been here eight years and have 12 more eternities of horror to serve.

Here I sit on a cane mat in an Asian prison cell, where fungus and moss grow off the walls, and sometimes off me, where my only light is a flickering, fading candle, where the insects of the night seek comfort from the rain and the dark, with me huddled around this one candle, where the rain itself can seem like a living, breathing creature. This seems like the whole universe to me.

My Spanish companion and friend, Antonio, died three days ago. He died slowly and in pain, but he did not die alone. He died in my arms.

Whose arms will I die in? I am now the last living white man in this world.

With every drop, dribble and splash, memories cascade through my mind, as does the rain gushing down the walls that surround me and the place where I am supposed to sleep.

How did I end up here? That is something I am still not 100 per cent sure about.

The prisoner in the next cell is a murderer. He's spent seven years in prison and is due to be released in August. 'Eddy the nun-killer' (as he is known) stabbed two nuns to death while robbing a church. The third nun who got in his way was slashed across the face with his bayonet, cutting open both her eyes and leaving her blind (a nun-killer, that's a bad *habit*).

The prisoner in the opposite cell is a sadistic cannibal. Buddha (as he is known) murdered his uncle, and to dispose of the body he did his bloody best to eat it. As time went against him, he only managed to eat the lungs, liver, heart and a bulk of his uncle's insides before his father started to ask where his brother was. As you can imagine, he was pretty pissed off to find out that his son was eating him.

Both Eddy and Buddha are pretty decent blokes, though. I've met worse in my short life.

Rain has a way of cleaning things: houses, streets, cars and in some cases memories (not to mention the floor of my cell). As the rain is tip-tapping on the roof and pouring through the bars of my cell, my thoughts tumble back. How did I manage to end up in this cesspit in the first place? The rain outside is an incessant tap-tap above me, and a torrent running in around me.

When the humidity here is at its peak you pray for the rain. When the rain comes and decides to stick around for a while, you pray for it to fuck off.

It's the memories of the past life that I have led that the rain brings so vividly to my mind.

CHAPTER I

BLEEDING WALLS

What is life
If all the risks
Are taken away?

My relationship with Sheryl stretched back to the early 1970s. Both born in Australia, we met in our teens, had our daughter Tammy in 1973, married in 1975, with a second daughter, Christina (Tina), born in 1982.

For many years, we had operated a successful stable and riding school in Kathmandu. We taught the children of foreign diplomats, privileged little Edward and Arabella, horseback riding and how to behave at a polo match.

The $50 per month from each of our 200 students amounted to big money for a couple of Australians living in a poor nation. We were comfortable, with money stashed in accounts in several Asian banks. But in 1984 our main bank went bankrupt and left us virtually penniless. The situation was so dire that I envied beggars in Bombay (at least they had a bowl to beg with).

The monsoon season hit Kathmandu, forcing us to close the school for

HELL'S PRISONER

two months. We had time to kill and needed to get away as a family, however nowhere seemed safe back in the early 1980s. In India, Indira Gandhi had just been assassinated and the country was in turmoil. The Sikhs were being slaughtered in their thousands after Sikh extremists had killed the prime minister with a machine gun, the assassins being none other than her own personal bodyguards (also Sikhs). One of them, named Mr Singh, had dedicated more than 30 years of his life to the protection of Indira Gandhi. Obviously religion and politics don't go hand-in-hand with loyalty or trust.

At a railway station in New Delhi, where I'd travelled to pick up my motorbike, more than 60 headless corpses were dragged onto the platform from a train, and yes, they were all Sikhs. When the news spread that the Sikhs were responsible for Indira Gandhi's death, Hindu passengers on the train had turned on them. There was nowhere for the Sikhs to run, they were butchered in their seats and in the aisles, their heads were hacked off then thrown out of the speeding train's windows.

Sri Lanka was also out of the question. The Tamils and the Sri Lankans were currently killing each other in religiously spawned, fanatical blood lust that had seemed to happen overnight. With just a dash of political poison the whole region, including Pakistan, was unstable. No Australian national, particularly one with a wife and two children, would step foot there without significant risk.

With barely enough money to get anywhere and stay a month, Sheryl and I decided to return to Australia via Indonesia.

On the night before we left Bangkok, Sheryl woke screaming, covered in sweat and trembling like a leaf. 'The walls, the walls, they're bleeding, they're bleeding, oh God, they're crying blood. There's blood all over me, the walls are crying,' she shrieked.

'It's OK, I'm here, I'm here, it's OK, I'm here,' I said, as I cradled her in my arms. 'It's only a bad dream, it's only a bad dream. I'm here, I'm here,' I repeated, as I gently rocked her.

'It's only a bad dream,' I whispered into her ear as she started to settle down, 'Nothing can hurt you while I'm here. It's OK, it's OK.'

I couldn't sleep; I was wide awake, locked in my own thoughts. I was 32 and Sheryl was 34. We wanted to go home and have a normal family life, but Sheryl was convinced that the entire world was trying to stop us.

'Something is always getting in our way,' she said. 'I feel it, something is trying to pull us apart and stop us from ever going home together.'

I'd felt it too but I did not let on.

It had been well over a decade since either of us had set foot in our own country. My eldest daughter Tammy, who was 12, had returned to Australia the previous year, after spending 11 of those years in Nepal. Sheryl and I had a few things to sort out between us and, once this was done, Sheryl and Tina were to go back to Australia.

I, on the other hand, was travelling with Sheryl and Tina to Bali then leaving them to head off to Australia while I travelled on to New Delhi.

My intentions were to sell up all of my business interests in Asia, India and the Orient, say goodbye to a few old friends, and return to Australia one month, possibly two at the max, after Sheryl had returned.

My family and I were accompanied by our friend Robert Campbell, or Doggie as he was affectionately known. Doggie was an Australian we had met in Kathmandu back in the late 1970s. As a constant visitor to Kathmandu, it was inevitable that over the years we would develop a close friendship. Doggie and some of his mates would occasionally rent my horses and guides for treks outside of the Kathmandu Valley, wanting to go up higher into the Himalayas. When Tammy travelled back to Australia, Sheryl and I trusted him enough to ask Doggie to accompany her and deliver her safely to my parents' home in Brisbane.

The flight to Bali was, as most flights are, full of plastic food and boredom. Clearing customs and immigration was reasonably brisk, but I can clearly remember a strange foreboding feeling striking me a number of times on the plane and during the one-hour taxi ride up to Ubud.

As I was a regular visitor to the Indonesian Islands, I had a small house (a *losman*) I had built for my family in Ubud that I would allow my friends to use when I wasn't there. Doggie had a losman in the same compound, next to mine.

When we arrived at the losman, I unhappily discovered that Ary Agung, the landowner, still had tenants in my place. The agreement I had with Ary when the place was built was that when I was out of the country the losman could be leased out. If I wished to utilise it I only had to give one week's notice prior to my arrival. To ensure no problems, I had forewarned Ary of my intentions *one month* prior to our arrival.

When I discovered there were people still residing in our losman, overtired and very annoyed I growled at Ary, 'When will it be ready?'

He said he had already made arrangements for a place for us to stay, until we could move back into our own losman.

As things worked out the people who were renting my place would be leaving the following morning anyway, so there seemed no harm done.

No problems, I thought . . .

With a beautiful crystal-clear night as our backdrop, Sheryl and I sat on the verandah of our temporary hotel and talked about starting over.

'I just want to go home, back to Australia,' she said, her eyes filling up with tears. 'Can't you see that? I just want to go home, I can't take any more of Asia.'

I watched as she collapsed in front of me, her face in her hands, heartfelt sobs escaping with each breath.

The silence between Sheryl's sobs was overridden by the sound of tiny footsteps.

Tina had wandered out from her bedroom and ever so gently put her fragile little hand in mine. My sweet, sweet four-year-old angel, I thought, Kathmandu was the only home she knew and there was nothing in that hotel that would have reminded her of the nursery back home in Nepal.

As my hand engulfed hers, she said, 'Daddy, let's go home, Mummy wants to go home!'

Unbeknownst to little Tina what Mummy meant was to return to her heritage. Sheryl was a tall exotic-looking quarter-caste Aboriginal girl – Australia was where her roots lay and it was there that she desperately wanted to settle.

I cuddled Tina and whispered, 'We will, I promise, if it kills me, if it costs me my life. We'll go and see your big sister who's with Nanna and Pappa. We're going to live in a gingerbread house and the fairies will come every day to play, to take your troubles away.' I made up a rhyme to make her feel better.

Sheryl wiped at her tears and said, 'That was the nicest, stupidest poem I've ever heard you make up, I bet you can't say it again?'

I'll take you to a gingerbread house, so put your faith in me,
I'll take you to a gingerbread house that no one else can see,
Where the fairies come to play each day,
To dance and sing your troubles away,
And that's the place where we will stay,
So put your faith in me.

We decided to call it a night and hit the sack – after all, tomorrow was a new day waiting to unfold.

Less than two hours later there was a knock on the door. Still jetlagged I dragged myself from the comfort of my bed, not to mention the comfort of my lady, wrapped in nothing but a sarong. As I opened the front door, Ary Agung appeared with a slimy look on his face.

'What's the problem?' I asked Ary.

'I've got some friends here,' he said.

The next thing I knew the place was full of police, over 18 of the bastards all waving and pointing handguns, pistols and rifles.

I was pushed up against a wall with half-a-dozen revolvers pointing at me from half-a-dozen directions. Sheryl was told to get out of bed and get dressed. The place was searched and when nothing illegal was found I was taken to the Kodak Police Station in Denpasar.

As I was being taken into a cell I saw Doggie sitting in handcuffs. As we exchanged quick glances, he gave a shrug of his shoulders as if to say, 'What the fuck's happening?' I returned the shrug as I was pushed along to the cell compound.

I was briefly questioned and then put in the police lockup until morning. Nothing else was asked of or said to me until that following day.

I spent the night surrounded by four old, stained, cracked and decrepit walls, heavy metal bars, no toilet and a cement floor for my bed (and toilet, I suppose).

After a sleepless night and a grumpy guard, whose idea of a wake-up call consisted of kicking an empty can down the corridor until it was beating against my cell door, it was 6.00 a.m. Time to be interrogated.

I was told to get up off the floor where I had been brooding. I was then handcuffed and taken into the police station offices, where I was sat down at a desk (physically).

The copper opposite me looked like an overweight monkey with a tie. Then it spoke. 'I am Captain Somaji Wouldyoulikeacigarette?' (well that's what it sounded like) he said, pushing a pack of those evil clove-filled *dotches* (cigarettes) towards me.

'It seems we have a problem here, drugs, and it appears that *you* are very deeply involved, we have the evidence, and we have the proof, so why don't you admit to your wrongful ways and accept the mercy of my country's courts,' he continued.

What shit's hit the fan here, I thought. Better play it by ear.

'Look, I am really quite confused, why have I been arrested?' I said.

'*Drugs*,' he replied. 'Drugs, your involvement in the drug trade and to help clear your confusion, my name is Captain Somaji Wouldyoulikeacigarette?' (Now I was really fucking confused!)

'Well, Captain Somaji Wouldyoulikeacigarette, I know nothing about the drug trade and even less about why I am here,' I stated.

That really got his little monkey's face working. He reached over pulling back his cigarettes and lit one up with his eyes locked on mine. I glanced over to the ashtray, where he still had one burning, then returned his stare.

'You will come with us,' he said.

I was loaded into a Toyota Land Cruiser and taken back to Ubud, where I met a frantic Sheryl.

We had little time to talk before the next Land Cruiser pulled up. Doggie was dragged out of it in handcuffs and we were then marched, or should I say dragged like a cat with shit on its paws, to Doggie's house, the front of which faced my own losmam!

'What's the go?' I said to Doggie as we were marched down the path that divided his losman garden and the one that I had.

'They've found the dope,' he mumbled.

'What fucking dope?' I asked with a gasp, as my eyebrows shot up to meet the back of my neck faster than Holland rollerblinds.

'No talking!' one of the coppers snapped as he broke us up.

I was then taken into the bathroom, or *mandi*, of Doggie's house and shown two statues.

Captain Wouldyoulikeacigarette stepped down into the sunken bath, and looked up at me. 'Please look,' he said, as he and one of his copper mates broke off the statues' bases.

When they had broken the statues away from their stands, the little monkey captain thrust his arms into the holes that were running up the centre of the statues and yelled, 'And what do you think of these?'

From where I was standing it looked like he was fist-fucking the statues, both audibly and visually, and getting off on this whole situation. He was breathing hard and even broke out into a sweat over it all.

'Don't lie, you know these holes and you know what they're for. You made them and you know what goes up inside them. So tell me, what have you got to say about these?' he said, as he stuffed each of his arms up and down the holes in the statues with a big shit-eating grin on his little monkey face.

'Well, if they're the type of holes that turn you on, which they appear to be doing, please enjoy. You sure do look like you're having a good time,' I said.

His face dropped. The smile vanished into a frown, then into a scowl as he looked down at his arms stuck up past the elbows in the statues. '*Diluar,*' he snapped at the other coppers who were all around me.

'*Diluar,*' he said again, which meant outside, and outside I was quickly shuffled to where four cardboard boxes were placed on the ground with Doggie standing in the distance, a look on his face of total despair.

When the little monkey copper captain managed to pull his arms out of the holes in the statues, he started to rant and rave about how the drugs were found in these holes. I had nothing to say because there was very little I could say.

We were all taken back to the Kodak Police Station, leaving Sheryl and Tina behind in Ubud.

When I was bundled out of the Land Cruiser I was taken into the office of the little monkey captain and had my handcuffs removed. As we sat down at his desk with me opposite (again), he said, 'So what have you got to say? You've seen the drugs, you've been to the house that you had paid for and you're guilty, so why don't you make a statement and let my country's mercy sentence you.'

'What did you say your name was?' I asked.

His shit-eating grin reappeared as he said, 'I am Captain Somaji Wouldyoulikeacigarette,' again pushing his filthy pack of dotches over towards me.

'Well, all I can say Captain Wouldyoulikeacigarette is, would you like a cigarette?' I said, as I pushed his cigarette pack back over to him with a smile on my face. 'I want a lawyer.'

'Mr smart man,' he growled, 'my name is Captain Somaji, not Wouldyoulikeacigarette. I speak very good English and if you wish to play games of words, then I too can play the game of words.' Then he stormed out of his office.

I was taken back to the lockup. The following day a bloke called Gary visited me from the Australian Council. He was about as helpful as an infected haemorrhoid. He looked at me as one would look at some oddity in a stool sample bottle.

His appearance was wrinkled, baggy and scruffy, though his clothes were well tailored. Above the collar line was a complete disaster.

He was in and out so quick I found myself hesitating to blink in case I missed him, though he did pause at the door on his hurried exit, saying, 'There are people coming from Jakarta to see you, it's best you talk with them.' Then he left.

I took that to mean the Australian Federal Police, operating out of their branch headquarters at the Australian Embassy in the Javanese capital, were on their way.

First problem: I'd entered Bali on a British passport.

Second problem: phoney passport.

CHAPTER 2

HELLO – IS THERE ANYBODY OUT THERE?

If sanity is a frame of mind
Then insanity must be
A mind without a frame

According to Immigration, and the passport I had stamped at Denpasar airport, my name was Russell Kenneth Duparcq (not a name my mother would have recognised).

During the 1970s and 1980s, holding multiple passports was a common practice among European, Antipodean and US citizens living throughout Asia. Certain passports guaranteed working visas in certain countries, while others may have allowed foreigners the right to buy and sell properties or establish businesses. Many US citizens, for instance, held fake Commonwealth, Canadian, British and Australian passports, which allowed them greater privileges in Commonwealth countries, like Hong Kong for example.

Well, this should be interesting, I thought. I entered the country under a British passport and now someone from the Australian Embassy in Jakarta is coming out to see me. I wonder who?

Before whoever it was from Jakarta could get out to see me, Sheryl had come to visit and she told me that Doggie had been released.

That really got me thinking. The fickle finger of give-ups was pointing at him and I started to think of a thousand ways to dispose of a human body, once you've boiled, grilled, baked and slowly simmered it. That's what I'd do to Doggie if he had given me up for something he may have been guilty of.

First I had to get out of this rotten bloody lockup. Sheryl had reasonably free access to me, but through all of her visits there was always someone there who could speak English. If we started to talk in Hindi or Nepali, the overhearing ears were left behind. We mainly spoke in English so that certain ears wouldn't get too suspicious or pissed off.

'I may have to make a run for it, Sheryl, so check out the courts. Maybe something can be arranged from there,' I said to her one day during a visit.

'What about me and Tina? If you escape, they'll throw us in jail,' she replied.

'Only if you're in the country when I do it, sweetheart,' I said placatingly, as she left to check out the Denpasar Court House.

When she had done what I asked of her, she returned a couple of days later with a smile on her sweet face. 'Easy,' she said. 'If you could get one of your mad mates waiting outside on a motorcycle, it wouldn't be all that hard. I've spent the last three days there watching and talking to other foreigners who are going to court there and I checked out the court room and toilets. There's a window in one of the toilets that leads out onto the street. The prisoners are allowed to use all of the toilets because there are only two of them anyway. So you could get out through the toilet window. Really easy and if there was a car, or better still a motorbike, you could easily get away. You'd have to get out of the country or at least off the island, but please don't try anything while I am in the country.'

Sheryl was a very clever and astute woman. We'd been together for a good 14 years and could often communicate without words. Sheryl wasn't anyone's fool, she was observant and quick, but now she was getting nervous. I quickly picked up on her feelings: they weren't much different to mine and I was shitting myself.

With great effort I suppressed a nervous breakdown and calmly said to her, 'Don't worry, just try to find out when I'm going to court. I still haven't been charged with anything yet, so there's a chance they may just turn around and release me. During the days you can't get in to see me, spend them at the court house and watch for any routine that they keep with the prisoners that are going to court, especially the foreigners. OK, sweetheart?'

'OK, sweetheart, but you won't try to escape while I am in the country with the baby, will you?"

When she returned a couple of days later she confirmed some of the stories that I had heard in the police station about drug convictions and their sentences. *Heavy.*

'I sat in court yesterday and you wouldn't believe it. Oh, Chris, they gave a German and an Italian death sentences,' she said, with eyes wide open, so beautiful in their innocence.

'And do they carry them out?' I asked.

'Gee, I was so shocked, I didn't ask,' Sheryl replied.

'Then you had better find out,' I said.

As our eyes locked, we both realised the seriousness of the whole situation. We knew there was a possibility that our entire future would be destroyed and that anything could happen.

'I will, I will,' she said as the copper came up to tell her that the ten minutes were up. 'But please don't do anything while I am in the country. Remember, I've got Tina.' And off she went.

Christ, here I am looking at a death sentence and she's worried about going to bloody jail. Women! I'll never understand them, or at least not that one. After a lifetime together how could she ever conceive the idea that I would leave her or any of my children in danger?

For the next three days I threw my mind into overdrive. When Sheryl visited me next, I told her to check out the mental asylum and when she returned to see me, a couple of days later, the news was good.

There had been a Swiss bloke who was arrested for drugs, half a kilo of heroin in fact, and he'd had a nervous breakdown. From what I had already heard in the police station, and from what Sheryl told me, if you're crazy they don't send you to jail or give you a death sentence. They ship you home to your country of origin.

As you can well imagine, my choices were limited.

I went crazy with a passion.

Every conceivably bent and twisted thing that a madman can do, that has ever been written down on a headshrinker's notepad, I did, and a lot more. I started by shitting in the two bags of rice they fed me each day.

I'd eat the food that the police would give me in the lockup, which was called Nasi Bunkus, or cooked rice in a bag, and then shit into the bag, neatly fold it and pack it against the wall.

Then I started walking around my cell with a pineapple under my arm, talking to it. I had made a face on it using two bottle tops stuck in sideways to represent eyes, its nose was only a hole with a piece of rag sticking out about two or three inches and, finally, it had two long plastic straws sticking up out of the top (for antennas). I called it Bent Benny – my advisor and friend.

Every time I was taken into the police office to be questioned I insisted that Bent Benny come with me. When Captain Somaji would ask me a question, any question, I'd consult Bent Benny first, which really pissed off Somaji.

'Look, I am just going to ask you a few simple questions. How do you feel?' he asked.

'Soft,' I replied, squeezing the pineapple that I'd had a stranglehold on for the past week. 'Soft, his pushbike is broken, everyone is holding back secrets, the colour blue is apple, the seeds have brought tickets to a porno movie, write 300 times "I will never wear a garter belt in the swimming pool",' I babbled on.

'Look, I only want to ask you a few questions and then you can return to your cell. How are you feeling?' Captain Somaji said again, with a death's head grin sprawled all over his uninviting face.

'Well, if that's the way you feel,' I said indignantly, 'Write 300 times "I will never wear a garter belt in the swimming pool",' and that got him going.

He ordered two other coppers to take Bent Benny off me, and what a mess that was. Benny absolutely disintegrated in all of our hands.

For the next week I sat on the floor of my cell teaching the cockroaches to come when I called them and, believe it or not, it only took a week. They seemed every bit as clever as the locals.

Whenever I rattled or crumpled any paper the cockies came out. I was just as amazed as the coppers to be honest. I never really thought you could teach cockroaches tricks. True as God, all I had to do was sit on the cell floor, rattle and crumple some paper in my hand and out they came from every hole, crack and crevice in that piss-arse cell. In fact, I even named some of them.

If I held out a little bit of food for them, they would come up and eat it out of my hand and let me pick them up without any fear in the world. I remember one morning when I was sitting on the floor feeding the cockroaches, from the corner of my eye I saw Captain Somaji standing at the cell door.

I pretended that I didn't see him and thought, how the fuck can I really blow his mind? I wanted him to think that the guy's so crazy, his brain needs an enema. Ah, the answer struck me and without thinking too much more I picked up the friendliest cockroach, which happened to be a big fat sucker.

'Oh, you're such a greedy big boy and greedy big boys have to be punished. Naughty, naughty, naughty,' I said, and quickly flicked the bastard into my mouth crunching down on it as fast as swallowed it. 'Now are there any other naughty boys h surveyed the floor, which was full of a good hundred cock all over the place.

The next morning I was given another pineapple so I made, or should I say created, Bent Benny II.

When Sheryl came to see me the next day, there were coppers all around her including Captain Somaji. She tried to talk to me as quietly as she could, throwing in Australian, American and Pommy slang words along with a few Hindi and Nepali words.

Somaji was right on the ball and I watched him carefully as Sheryl said, 'Did you really eat a cockroach? Christ, you're not really going mad, are you?'

That's when I realised that if I could make her believe that I was out of my tree I could trick anyone. I said to her through the cell bars, 'I've got someone you have to meet, he's my best mate, wait here and I'll get him.'

With that I turned around and pulled out a piece of paper and sat down on the floor.

Those cockies were well trained, and within five minutes I had the team out. I picked up one and said, 'Gabriel, Gabriel, this is my wife, she's come all the way from Brazil to meet you, here.' I offered it to Sheryl.

Everyone stepped back from the cell door, including Sheryl, as I held out the cockie (who by now was kicking up a stink as I held it by the legs, its wings flapping every which way).

'Don't be naughty, Gabriel, Gabriel, Gabriel!' I said, acting as though I was getting all pissed off. I didn't have to act much, that little Gabriel was pissing me off, so I bit the little bastard in half, swallowing the first bit and offering the other half to Sheryl.

Sheryl went white from shock, and that's putting it mildly – her face dropped like a ton of bricks as she started to scream, 'He needs a doctor, he needs a doctor! My God, my husband needs a doctor.'

'Oh no,' I said to all the startled faces standing at my cell door, 'he's OK, I can put him back together; watch,' and I ate the other half of Gabriel (he kicked like shit all the way down my bloody gullet, the little bludger).

Two weeks later, I was transferred to the Bungli Mental Asylum. Man what a trip that was! Have you ever tried to play Jack Nicholson? Have you ever been in the 'Cuckoo's Nest'? It's not only hard, it's off the planet! I should know, I've been there.

I was dragged out of the Denpasar Police Station in the early hours of the morning by a team of coppers and blokes in dirty white gowns. All the blokes in the dirty white gowns were armed with needles, and all the coppers were trying to hold some part of my body down for them to shoot me up with syringes that looked like rusty nails.

I fought like a madman, gone madder, because no one had told me where I was being taken to at the time, or what was in those scabby-looking needles they were trying to impale me with.

All I can clearly remember is Captain Somaji watching with a look of terror on his face as I smashed and kicked, my fingers almost superglued to my pineapple. I screamed out: 'Beam me up Spock, beam me up Spock, Spock.' I screamed into my pineapple, 'Beam me fucking up,' as I felt a dozen, no ten dozen, needles striking home. My last real conscious thought was, 'Shit, they've od'ed [overdosed] me. Beam me up Spock.'

The only saving grace was when Doggie turned up out of the blue. Christ, what a sight for sore eyes that man was.

When I came to, I was firmly installed in the Bungli Mental Asylum, strapped to a bed. My first thought was, 'Spock . . . Spock . . . Christ, who's Spock?'

My mind started to clear as I realised where I was. Another fine mess you've gotten us into, Ollie, I thought, and started to laugh. I don't know what they shot me up with, but whatever it was, it was *goooooood*. I was the happiest bloke in the world for the next two days, laughing and giggling every time I shat or pissed myself.

Sheryl was allowed to visit me but as my head cleared, so too did the distance between us grow.

I was given needle after needle, tablet after tablet whilst strapped to that rotten cot. How could I fight? Once unstrapped I was a lot less vulnerable, so as you can imagine the medication was eventually reduced to zero.

'*Buka*' and '*minum*' became two words I would learn immediately as the guards, who were also the nurses, dealing out the so-called medication would visit me anywhere between 6 and 10 times over a 24-hour period.

They would use these two words repeatedly ('buka, buka', meaning 'open, open', and 'minum, minum', meaning 'drink, drink'), as they shoved the little red acid-like tablets into my mouth and pushed the cup up to my lips.

It proved to be tough, keeping up the facade of a mental patient and suffering the side effects of the mind drugs that were so liberally dispensed, without actually taking them. Assuming that I was just as fucked up as every other basket case in the joint, the guard would do a less than thorough check of my mouth using a paddlepop stick, or should I say, *the* paddlepop stick.

Remember, this was an Indonesian mental asylum, not a Western doctor's surgery, and the same paddlepop stick was used to explore the mouths, stretch the lips, and probe the tongues of every snot-encrusted, disease-infested inmate within the walls of this menagerie of the mad.

In order to not lose the plot completely, I mostly hid the tablets under my tongue and patiently waited for the guard to move on before spitting them into my hand and then burying them in any crevice I could find in my cell.

By the time Doggie turned up my mind was as clear as could be expected; however, I had to play the space case when Sheryl and Doggie came together.

I only got a chance to talk to Doggie when Sheryl pissed off to do things like clean the cell that I had been moved to and arrange for the cleaning and airing of the clothes and bedding I was given.

'Get me out of here, fucker. I don't care how you do it, but get me the fuck out of here,' I said to Doggie.

'Haven't you gone mad?' Doggie asked, as his eyebrows flew up in amazement as though he had just heard his socks break out in conversation.

'Yeah, I'm as mad as a hatter, as mad as you for coming back here, which was totally stupid. Why did you do it?' I said.

'I heard that you had gone around the bend after I left, so I changed my brief, grabbed all the cash I could beg borrow and steal, and came back to see what I could do to help you and get Sheryl and Tina out of the country,' Doggie replied.

'Why did they release you, Doggie?' I asked. 'And why the fuck was there dope in your house? What were you up to, mate?'

'Well that's a long story, mate,' he said.

'And you know how to make a long story short, arsehole, you cut off the tail. So tell me how the fuck did that dope end up in your . . . Christ, here comes Sheryl. She still thinks I am out of my tree, so let's keep it that way. She's got this thing about going to jail and I don't fancy death sentences. Have you heard?' I said, and changed the subject as Sheryl drew near.

'Bent Benny didn't sprock, but he had his garter belt. Gabriel doesn't like swimming pools,' I babbled.

Doggie's eyebrows lifted as the conversation so drastically changed along with my manner of speech.

'What's that?' he asked, as she drew closer.

'That guy over there, he's got cotton wool, but he never shares it. But I know where there are two coloured pencils. You want to see them, come on, come on,' I said, as I pulled on Doggie's arm.

Doggie looked over at Sheryl and she smiled her best matronly smile.

'Humour him, Doggie, go and see his two coloured pencils. I still want to get one of the lazy bastards to clean out the drain where he's supposed to shit. All the shit just gets washed down into his cell. It's bloody disgusting. I want to get him moved up into the top cell where the shit doesn't get washed down – it's hard to wash shit uphill,' she said, starting to crack up at her own dud joke.

She was right – there were nine single cells that ran down one side of the block that I was in. You had to shit, piss, vomit or whatever in this open drain on the floor against the back of the wall. The whole drainage system was built sloping down, so the sewerage from the first cell would run down into the last cell where it was cleaned away once a week.

As luck would have it, this last cell had my name on it for a whole shitty week.

'Go and check out his coloured pencils, but watch him,' Sheryl said, and off I went, dragging Doggie down the corridor.

'What colours are your pencils, mate?' Doggie asked, all happy and childlike, as we moved away from my cell – or caged-in room – that Sheryl was supervising the cleaning of.

'What?' I asked.

'Your pencils, what colour are they?' he said with a nerve-streaked smile.

'Black and blue, fuckhead, the colour of your eyes if you don't help me get out of this fucking finger-painting paradise,' I said.

'Settle down, mate, what the fuck is happening between you and Sheryl?' he asked.

I filled him in on the fact that if I could fool her, I could fool anyone.

A week later Doggie had arranged everything. The only intrusion was that of my younger brother, Shane. I kept up the farce with him the whole time. It was decent of him to come to try and help me out, but there was really nothing that he could do to help me. He didn't know Asia and he had no contacts; in fact, it was his first time out of Australia. It was best that he was sent home while Doggie and I played the game.

Everything was prepared for my escape out of the asylum. Passports, cars and motorcycles; it was foolproof.

I had been on my best behaviour as far as you can expect a nutter to be. I wasn't violent. The violent cases were kept in a block that ran opposite to the block that I was in.

I was being held in a long building that on one side had single cells for maximum security, and on the other side had caged-in rooms where they kept the run-of-the-mill maniacs in groups of 10 and 20. Because my cell door faced the larger cells I could stand at the door dribbling and slobbering all down my shirt and still watch the daily shows, and learn from them. That's how I learned to dribble and slaver so well.

I was spitting up the drugs that they were giving to me as fast as the grinning meat-faced giggling nurse would piss off. You know, sometimes I would wonder just who was the craziest, the nurses or the patients? It must be an occupational hazard, I decided. Hanging out with all these bent bastards must rub off. I found myself doing some pretty weird things even when no one was looking.

The drugs that were being stuffed down the throats of the patients quicker than the poor pricks could yawn were deadly. They were all basically mind drugs, the worst of which was the Fluphenazine. The pills are little red-coloured buggers and are as bitter as shit. I'd already known about this drug from a previous experience I'd had in Kathmandu, when a New Zealand bloke I knew flipped out and was loaded up with the shit so that he could be controlled to be flown back to New Zealand. It affects not only the way you talk, but also you can't even walk after you've been stuffed with this shit. You can only lift your feet a few inches when you walk, more like a shuffle – I called it the 'Fluphenazine Shuffle' – and your tongue has a way of falling out of your face with a life of its own.

The day came when the Chinese–Indonesian headshrinker came to check me out, and there I was dribbling and drooling in fine form as I stood at the cell door shuffling away. I had been trying to outdo the bloke in the opposite cell, who had been standing there for half of the morning looking at me, hobbling away on the spot and covering the bars in spit, saliva, snot and whatnot.

Not to be outdone, I let my nose run more than usual instead of sniffing it back (thankfully I'd been inflicted with the flu). I dribbled and drooled for all I was worth. Snot, spit and phlegm were flowing fountain-like from my face.

'Ah, you look well today,' the Chinese–Indo headshrinker said.

Christ, I thought, I must look like the loser of a fucking snot fight with an elephant. If I'd been wearing socks they'd have been soaked!

'Yes, you look very well today, tomorrow you can go out and exercise in the sun with your friend,' he said with a well-practised smile as he nodded at the heavy competition I had across the hall, and off he moved to the next cell.

Competition proved to be tough as I stared across at the quivering piece of phlegm, shaped to resemble a human.

Great, thinks I, if I can only keep the spit and snot flowing, I've got a chance. If I was to be allowed to go for walks, or at least shuffles, in the exercise yard, I had a good chance of getting out of here. So once a day I would be taken out for a shuffle with all my fellow shufflers.

The plot was starting to form and if Doggie could be relied on I wouldn't have to spend months, if not years, in the asylum.

The old sixth sense was warning me that if I went through the Indo court system, and some arsehole like Captain Somaji was handling the case, I'd get shafted. After all, from my own experience, Indonesia has a 100 per cent conviction record – if you go to court you get convicted. In fact, the head judge at my case had stated to the Australian consul: 'Indonesia's police do not arrest innocent people . . . if they arrest you . . . you must be guilty, therefore you must be sentenced.'

When Doggie came to visit me I explained that the best time to go was during the shuffle exercises, so we formulated my escape.

Doggie arranged for everything on the outside. All I had to do was be next to the wall of the asylum exercise yard at the right time.

The day that everything was set up for me to go, it rained and none of the patients were taken out for their daily shuffle. I spent that day screaming with the rest of my mates there, but I had something to really scream about, as my freedom was being delayed.

The following day, it rained again so I led the chorus in fucking screaming!

When the nurses turned up, and because I saw them coming, I had the good sense to shut up and do some serious dribbling.

'Who started this? Who started this?' one of the nurses screamed out, waving his leather sap in the air (which was filled with sand).

When the other patients saw who it was they all shut up and joined me in some serious dribbling and drooling. After all, this so-called nurse was known as Ming the Merciless, the cruellest little dog-shit nurse of them all, who would rather bash the shit out of a patient than go and collect his pay cheque. Ming the Merciless was more bent than any of the patients.

Everyone shut up, except one total imbecile who kept screaming. Ming homed in on him and shut him up real sharp. When the nurses left the wing of the building, with Ming smiling as though he had just won the lottery, the last screamer was strapped to his steel cot, babbling and drooling like all the rest of his cellmates – only he was feeling worse.

The following morning we were taken out for our exercises and I was fit to burst. It didn't rain, though all my fellow patients were matching the heaviest of showers as the saliva flowed freely from their drooping, drooling mouths.

They were happy, but not as happy as me. There were roughly thirty of us in the exercise yard and you'd go far to find a happier bunch of head cases. Doggie had said that he would keep returning to the outside wall for a couple of days if I should run into any problems.

I leaned back on the inside exercise wall that separated me from the free world, thinking of the street on the other side that would take me there.

I just kicked back, scratching my crotch, picking my nose, dribbling and drooling, waiting for the message or the sound that would tell me that Doggie was outside.

I was propped up against the wall when I casually glanced down at one of my fellow dribbling compatriots. He had just discovered his prick, or so it seemed. He had his mork stork in his hand and was checking it out as if for the first time. He picked up a small twig and started to poke at it, like it was some type of dead lizard or bird he had just found and wanted to see if it was still alive.

It's strange how the macabre attracts people's attention – well it does me, and most of the people I know. Try as I may, I couldn't stop looking back down at this nutter pushing the twig down the eye of his prick. Christ I thought, that must really fucking cane. The twig he was forcing down the 'throat of his plucked duck' was about the size of a pencil, though not nearly as smooth. It had half a dozen or more smaller out-shoots poking out its sides that he had broken off, but not very neatly.

I kept trying to look away, but couldn't help looking back to the nutter as he chuckled, laughed and then screamed out, 'Ouch, ouch, ooh, ooh.' He would start to laugh again, as his prick began to harden. There he was with a twig sticking out the end of his erection, looking like some barbarian flagpole. At the time, it was one of the weirdest things I'd ever seen.

Bent bastard, I thought, as I pulled a boogie out of my nose and checked it out . . . Shit, that was a big one, I thought, as I wiped it off on the shoulder of a passing inmate, who was sincerely pleased by the gift.

Come on, Doggie, get your shit together, I thought.

The next thing I knew one of the other twisters was nudging me and pointing at the bloke sitting down beside me. When I looked down, the nutter was having a wank, without a care in the world, just 'pullin' his pud', the dirty little bastard.

One of the other patients wandered over to check it out, then looked at his own prick, then back to the little bastard who appeared to be having such a good time. His eyes fell back to his stork once more and there seemed to be an audible clank, as his mind registered what the bloke on the ground was doing. Within seconds he was savagely pulling on his own jatz cracker.

I thought, by Christ, he's going to pull the fucking thing off.

Within 15 minutes, over 60 per cent of the lads in the exercise yard had a good grip on themselves.

When the nurses returned to check on their keep, they discovered that there was a massive surge of mass masturbation.

Just before the nurses returned, that 60 per cent quickly jumped to about three in every four patients all stroking away or in the process of pulling their dirty dicks out.

Still, there were others who had already blown their load and were wiping their hands in other patients' hair, or staring at their cum-saturated hands as if they had just discovered their first true love.

Christ, I thought, if they all start wanking like this, what will I do? Some pretty wild and weird thoughts then ran through my head . . . fucken' oath, I'll have a wank if that's what I have to do to keep up with these crazy fuckers. In fact I'll go one better, I'll pull my dick out and run around the exercise yard singing, yes that's what I'll do, and what will I sing? Instantly these words jumped into my mind:

I'll wave my willy at the world each day
Cause being mad's the game I play
So I'll wave my willy at the world and say
Luck's not gonna fuck me today.

Christ, I thought, I'm going mad. Though looking back, it sure must have looked pretty weird and wild to the guards when they finally did return. I now laugh to myself at the bizarre thoughts that I entertained on that day.

The guards were all pissed off, probably because no one asked them to join in on the fun.

We were marched back to our cells. I was the last patient to leave the exercise yard with three guards behind me.

As I stepped through the doorway, back into the hospital block, the last sound I heard was, 'Beep, beep, beep,' the pre-arranged signal that Doggie was outside waiting for me. I nearly cried.

The patients finished up their party, all laughing and giggling with the occasional sperm-covered hand cleaning itself on the walls of its cell.

I was on the verge of tears as I was locked back into my cell, and it must have shown on my face because one of the English-speaking nurses said to me, 'Did they upset you? Don't be upset, they're dirty, dirty boys and only dirty, dirty boys play with themselves, and you're not a dirty little boy, you don't play with yourself, do you? You're not a dirty little boy,' he said and off he rushed, with a million-dollar smile on his face, to join Ming the

Merciless, and all of the other nurses, in the bashing and whacking of some of their wayward wanking wards.

You dickhead, I thought, I'd stand up and choke the chicken on top of Queen Elizabeth's fucking dining table while she was giving a bloody speech and a reception if I thought it would get me out of here, but not when I'm expecting Doggie on the other side of the fucking wall. Or would I?

Anyway, bash those bastards, smash the rotten little jerk-offs, I thought as I watched the nurses tearing into those half-wit, dog-arsed, prick-pulling, pissed-pants patients. Give me a stick, my kingdom for a stick and a free go at those arseholes you're thrashing and I'll show you how it's done. As you can imagine, I was pissed off because of those bent arseholes with their fucking fists of fury, for I was set back once again.

CHAPTER 3

THE DEMON SHOWS ITS FACE

I am coming from forever
And I am going to the end

The following day was raining when I woke up, so naturally I woke up feeling bad. When I heard from one of the nurses that Sheryl had come to visit me, I started dribbling.

'Doggie said that he tried to visit you but, because of the rain, you probably weren't allowed visits. You know what Doggie's like, he'll try again. So how are you feeling today? You look as handsome as ever,' she said, when she came to see me.

My first thought was, is she relaying a message? Has Doggie been around these last few days in the rain to help me get the fuck out of here? Has he confided in Sheryl? Well, if he has or hasn't, there's not much that I can really do about it but try again and check my lady Sheryl out.

'Did Doggie really come to try to see me?' I said, dribbling.

'Well he's come back all wet the past two days. He sure had been somewhere,' she replied.

'Did he tell you where he went?' I said, still dribbling the best I could, trying not to look at her.

Her eyes locked onto mine and I couldn't look away, we just started to stare at each other.

'You're not really mad, are you?' she said.

I said nothing, but her eyes were still locked onto mine.

'You've only been playing a game, you're planning to try to escape. How stupid I've bloody been. I should, by God I should . . . '

Her eyes started to sink deeper into my own.

'What should you do, my little lady? Should you cage the beast, or cage the bird? Should you sell your soul for mountains of gold and freedom if you can, for this one stupid man?' I said.

'You're crazy,' she said. 'You're crazy.'

About half an hour later she had bribed the guards, or should I say nurses, to take me out for a shuffle in the exercise yard.

I scuffled around for a good ten minutes and when the nurses were satisfied with that Sheryl came out into the empty exercise yard and sat down on a bench.

I sat beside her and neither of us spoke. When I heard the three-beep signal, or better described as three dots, three dashes, three dots, I looked at her and kissed her on the lips.

'I love you, sweetheart, I love you,' I said, and off I ran across the exercise yard and up the drainpipe that I had seen two or three other patients swing off. I was up that pipe faster than a rat up any drainage pipe.

When I got to the gutter of the building I flipped myself over onto the roof, but, as I did so, I felt the guttering falling away.

My mind was in overdrive. The guttering is too weak, I thought. Find the apex of the roof and run along that. More people will see you up there, but fuck it, besides it's got to be stronger than this rotten gutter. So off I scampered up to the apex of the roof, climbing like a monkey on speed.

I was kicking out tiles left, right and centre. But once I got myself up onto the top of the roof, I started to walk across it like a tightrope-walker. The closer I started to get to the middle of the roof, the more it started to bend. It's strong enough, I reassured myself, so I kept up the steady pace.

As I reached the centre of the building and I could see Doggie, my face burst into a big grin and so did his. All I had to do was make it across this last part of the roof and I was free!

That's when the first cement tiles started to give way. I felt them loosening rapidly beneath my feet. I had no choice but to stick with the centre beam. Unfortunately, the centre beam of any building is the one that crosses the roof, which generally holds up the tons of tiles. My luck on that day was on holiday.

I started to fall through the bloody thing. The whole roof gave way. As I fell through it, grabbing onto wooden beams and breaking tiles, I could see Doggie's smile fade.

'Come on, come on, come on, mate, come on,' he cried.

'Fuck off, fuck off, mate, fuck off,' I screamed, as I fell through the roof right into the middle of the violent offenders' block.

This block was where they kept the lowest of the low of human existence. The inmates had fingernails like the claws of wild animals. The dirt was ingrained into their skin, their hair a filthy mat of excrement, twigs and dead bugs; their clothes were rags you wouldn't wipe shit off your shoes with. Their faces were those of the completely insane, dirt-encrusted, some with slight beards, others covered with hair, but all with the same mad eyes.

Bare footed, they looked like something you'd find in the primal caves of a lost or forgotten world. The dirt was embedded into their feet, and their toenails so long and sharp they resembled the talons of a Neanderthal or a Cro-Magnon man.

This was definitely not the best place in the world to just drop into and I wasn't really prepared for the reception when I landed on the floor.

Those who were chained up could only growl, yell or scream. The rest came in for the kill. They were onto me faster than the Yanks make up foreign policies, and my dropping into their block like that could only mean one thing. 'Hey, twisters, dinner is served!'

I found myself being bitten, clawed, scratched and mauled by a good dozen mindless teeth and hands. What a fucking rotten place to die, I thought, as the twisters all fell upon me.

A wild voice screamed out in my mind, 'Stand and you live, fall and you die.'

'Fuck me!' I screamed at the top of my lungs (with no literal intention of the word), as a wild and totally insane part of me seemed to take over, filling me with an incredible strength. 'Kill the fuckers,' this demon voice screamed from within.

I not only knew it was going to be them or me, I felt it. A sense of fear surged through me, numbing my entire body for split seconds. Blood boiling and adrenalin now taking over, the taste of freedom still fresh on my tongue, anger erupted, replacing whatever fear I had.

As I lashed out, frozen images of Doggie's desperate plea flashed through my mind, like when our eyes locked for that brief second – 'C'mon, c'mon, mate' – with the look of terror reflecting what appeared to be a mirror image of my own fear-stricken face.

Anger rose in me like a giant black tsunami, with seemingly all its power. I punched, hit, scratched and clawed, spat, bit and kicked my way to the nearest safe wall so none of these crazed inhumane creatures could get behind me.

Somehow I managed to get hold of a steel bedpost during the mêlée. Completely enraged, I quickly stepped in and out using the metal bar as my weapon against the much slower, Fluphenazine-shuffling imbeciles.

The walls were splattered with blood when the nurses finally arrived. I was standing in the middle of the room in a frenzy, still clenching the bar in my bloodied hands. My mind had actually gone over the top. Kill me here I thought, but I will surely drink your blood first, you fuckers.

The nurses seemed to read my thoughts, as they stepped away.

Sheryl walked in and as she did her expression changed to one of horror as she stared at me. 'The walls of blood! The walls of blood! I've seen them before, they're the walls of blood that I dreamed of. The walls are bleeding,' she said. 'This is what I dreamed about.'

I moved forward and looked up to the walls and they were bleeding. They were crying blood. Is this her dream, I thought? It all seems so real.

Then my lights went out, as one of the nurses sapped me.

When I came to, I was strapped to my cot. The first voice that I could recall was that of Sheryl saying, 'Don't hurt him, don't hurt him, he doesn't know what he's doing,' then off I faded into never-never land again, to dream of a Bangkok hotel room that cried blood. When I awoke from that bad dream I was shipped back to the Denpasar Police Station.

Captain Somaji had filed a report that said I had tried to escape Bungli Mental Asylum so, for security reasons, I was returned to police custody.

On our last visit, after I had stopped pretending that I was a space case to Sheryl, she said to me, 'Did you really go a little bit crazy?'

'Aren't I always?' I said.

'Yeah, I suppose you always were. That's probably why I love you so much and could never love anyone else in the same way as I love you,' she replied with a smile.

'But, you'll learn,' I said, as my fingers softly caressed the golden ringlets of young Tina's hair through the bars of the lockup.

'You'll learn to love someone else. Life is like that, you love or hate what you have, and when it's gone you only love or hate it more. Goodbye, my sweet tall lady,' I said, as I pulled her face towards mine, kissing away the tears that were flowing down her cheeks.

'You're not as tough as you pretend to be, are you?' I said.

'I am tough enough when I have to be,' she said.

'That's good news, now you really need to be tough,' I said, as I pushed her away. 'You were always an arsehole in my eyes and I never really ever loved you,' I said softly.

'Neither have I, you piece of shit,' she said huskily, holding back her tears, as the copper came to break up our last visit. 'I feel nothing for you, you, you stupid, stupid arsehole. I don't love you any more. Do you understand? Do you understand? I don't love you any more,' she softly growled, as if angry.

'And I don't love you,' I said, through the bars of the lockup.

'I never have, and I never will, and I'll never stop these feelings,' she said.

As Sheryl was led away from my cell, she broke from the copper's grip and ran back to the cell where I was and pulled my face to hers and, as our lips met, she said, 'I'll always love you, you're a special part of my life, just as I am a special part of yours. I love you, you stupid thing and I always will,' she said and off she ran to her new life.

A life in the West, while I stayed behind to write the words that you now read.

Clang, Clink, Clink, Clang, Clang, Clink.

'Shit! Why can't God just give us water in Aqua bottles, instead of all this rain?' I thought, as I started to dry myself off.

Peeling off my encrusted socks, I said to myself, 'Son, you're the original cabbage head. When they took off your shoes, why didn't you use your brain?'

Because I thought they would give them back.

Ah! That shows just how stupid you are, you fuckwit.

Now, now don't start that again, you're in the shit so take it as it comes and sooner or later something will turn up and you can get the fuck out of here.

Yeah, yeah, yeah, replied that little voice in the back of my mind. You've been saying that for the past five months and here you are wetter than Moby's dick, you dickhead.

You should have done the bolt when you made that fucking key out of the mozzie stand and had the lock undone in the lockup – that was your golden chance and you blew it.

The guard woke up so I had to re-lock the bloody thing.

No you didn't, you could have jumped him, you could have turned the fucker's lights out and fucked off with his gun and his wallet, said that little devil voice inside my head.

Oh yeah, and then where would I have gone? To the airport without money, passport, or dollars? With all of the Balinese police force looking for a white cop-killer? No thank you.

Weak shit, you wouldn't have had to kill him, just put him out of action, that's all.

Yeah, easy to say, but once I am out with a gun in my hand, I'd go dog shit.

I can beat these charges – they're shit – so relax and see what tomorrow brings. Yeah, just take it easy and wait for tomorrow.

I had spent the last five months in either a foreign police lockup, where they were talking a language that I couldn't understand, or a mental asylum. I ended up talking to myself.

Have you ever talked to yourself? If you say you haven't, well all I can say is that you're lying. We all talk to ourselves, though most of us won't admit it, and if you do that for as long as I did you start to answer yourself.

After arguing with myself, I discovered that there are two sides, not only to me, but to everybody. There was one side of me that was pretty straight and easygoing, and the other side was a total prick. It was the wild side that kept getting me into trouble.

You could say that I had started to learn more about myself, and I was bent, I thought, because I could talk to myself in my own mind.

I was still arguing with myself as I was pulling off my socks when I heard an Australian voice yell out, 'Hey mate, hey you, do you speak English?'

'Yeah, a little,' I replied.

'Hey, are you that Aussie bloke that we've been expecting these past few months? We thought that you had bought your way out. What the fuck are you doing here?' he said.

'I'm not sure, I thought that they were just after a quid or two, but it seems that they want some blood. What's your name?' I replied.

'Sam, I am an Australian. What's yours?'

'Russell, and I speak English, it's my mother tongue,' I said. (From the first day in Denpasar Police Station I knew that for the moment, Christopher ceased to exist.)

'Hey, catch this ball,' Sam said, and he bounced a ball towards the cell door. The first time he missed, the second time I caught it.

'Have you got it?' he asked.

'Yeah, I've got it,' I replied.

It was a tennis ball attached to a string and, as I pulled it towards my cell, I could see a black plastic bag attached to it. When I had pulled the bag into my cell, Sam yelled out, 'Welcome to Krobokan Prison.'

The bag was filled with *arak*, which is the local firewater. To me it seemed more like paint stripper, and just the smell of it nearly made me spew. Christ, I thought, the man who drinks this shit has a death wish.

I snookered the poison next to the squatter shitter and started to check out my surroundings.

It took less than five minutes to check the place out – dirty walls, dirty floors, dirty ceiling, shit-encrusted squatter and paint peeling from the rusty bars on the windows and doors.

'Hey, mate, what did you say your name was?' Sam called out, with a slur.

'Russell,' I replied.

'Whereabouts in Australia are you from?' he asked.

From then on, we started to talk the night away. It felt good talking to a fellow countryman once again, although I avoided most questions he asked about me and kept guiding the conversation back to him, how he was arrested and how many other foreigners were in the prison.

'There are 14 other Aussies here, a couple of Kiwis, quite a few Euros too. Hey you, frog dog, wake up, you ugly prick,' he yelled out, as he picked up a stick and started bashing it on the bars of the next cell.

A couple of minutes later a voice started mumbling something in French that didn't sound anything like 'Gee, thanks for waking me up.'

When the French bloke dragged himself to his cell door he looked over towards me, smiled, showing all his rotten black broken teeth, and said, '*Bonjour.*'

'Don't Bonjour the cunt,' Sam said. 'Say G'day like I taught you, you frog dog.'

'Ah, *oui, Gadday,* mate,' the Frenchie said, 'and who have I the honour of being woken up to meet?'

'He's Russell and he's a fucking Aussie. At this rate if they keep busting fucking Australians, there will be no one left in Australia to turn the fucking lights off,' Sam growled, as he picked up a mug the size of a small bucket and had a few huge swigs.

The shit that he was drinking was pouring down his cheeks, as were his tears.

'Fucking arseholes, I want to go home,' he yelled, as he staggered to his mattress on the floor. 'I just want to go home . . . Bastards, they're all bastards . . . Bastards, fucking bastards . . . ,' he mumbled, then began to grumble and groan until snores took over.

The Frenchie shrugged his shoulders and once again smiled. 'My name is Phillipe. Would you like a drink?' he said, as he reached to the floor to pick up a mug, which I am sure was the brother of the one that Sam was using to splash his face with before he passed out on his mattress.

'No thanks, mate, I've already got one,' I replied.

So I spent an hour or so talking with the Frenchie, until the dawn was starting to lighten up our cells, when we both bid each other 'Good Morning' and tried to catch a few winks before the cells were unlocked.

That morning we were all let out of our cells at 6.00 a.m., and at 7.00 a.m. there was an *appell* – a head count – of the prisoners in each block.

When the guards came around, we were expected to line up outside our cells as they ticked us off on their clipboards.

After the guards had gone, my cell was flooded with the other foreign prisoners who came to introduce themselves to the new foreigner on the block – me.

There were a heap of Aussies, ranging from skinny little James Cook, who looked like an out-of-work jockey, to Warren Smith, who looked like a wayward Conan. Warren was built like a brick shithouse, but with a lower IQ. There were Dutch, French, German, English, Swiss, a half-caste Algerian–Swede, Italian, Spanish, a bloke from Lapland (no one knew where he really came from because he only had Japanese passports . . . 42 of them), a couple of Japanese and of course Kiwis and Australians. Quite a mixed lot if nothing else.

It took me a month or so to settle in and get to know the other foreign prisoners and find out which guards were 100 per cent arseholes and which ones were only 99 per cent arseholes, not too mention which of the local prisoners were cool and which ones were dogs; 99.9 per cent of them were dogs.

As the months went past, I found my own little niche in the place as I waited to go to court. I was pretty confident that I would beat all the charges that were filed against me. After all, no hashish was found on me, no hashish was found in the room I had been renting, so what did I have to worry about? All I could really do was wait and be cool.

My first shock came when James Cook came back from court charged with transporting 32 grams of hashish, for which he was given 17 years.

A couple of days later, Guiseppe the Italian and Willy the German both came back with death sentences. They had been appealing.

This was wrong, absolutely wrong, I thought. Don't panic, they can't convict me, I was clear. I had nothing to fear – after all, I thought, I've only been charged with suspicion.

Christ, suspicion, what sort of a brumby charge is that? No, they will never convict me, I reassured myself, but deep down I was terrified.

When I made my first appearance in court, I started to worry more than a worried person should worry.

The police had supplied 22 witnesses to give evidence against me – 20 of them I didn't know from a bar of shit. I'll not go into the nitty-gritty of it all, but I will mention a few of the highlights.

Ninety per cent of the witnesses admitted that the first time they saw me was when the police showed them a photograph of me. 'Why,' I asked through the court-appointed interpreter, 'did the police show you a photograph of me?'

'Oh, so we wouldn't make any mistakes in identifying you when we were in court,' they all said.

When I complained about this to the judge, he replied, 'This is normal police procedures here in Indonesia. It's standard police techniques and tactics, so please sit down.'

I was told that when I was questioned I could only reply yes or no to the court. Then the judge asked me, 'Is it true that you entered the country with your wife and child? Is it true that you entered the country on a British passport? Is it true that you are now being held in remand at Krobokan Prison? Is it true that you are a drug dealer and smuggler, and is it true that the drugs found in Ubud at the Fibra Inn were yours?'

'Well, your honour, I did enter the country with my wife and . . .' I began.

But before I could say any more, the judge yelled out, 'I only want a simple and single yes or no, don't confuse this court with your stories. Just a simple and single yes or no.'

'But, your honour, you've asked me a number of questions, please let me explain,' I replied.

'You'll have plenty of time for that later, but now I only want a simple and single yes or no, is that clear?' the judge responded.

I looked at my lawyer and he stood up and said something in Indonesian that I couldn't understand.

He then said to me, 'If the questions get too tricky, I'll write the answers down on this piece of paper, OK.'

'Yeah, OK, so what should I say now?' I asked.

He pulled out a felt pen and wrote no comment on the back of a folder he was holding, so when the questions were repeated to me, I replied, 'No comment.'

For the next 28 appearances in court, whenever I was asked a question or should I say questions, I would look over towards my lawyer and he would flash the back inside cover of his folder and I would reply, 'No comment.'

When it came time for my lawyers (I had two of them) to cross-examine a witness, they would always reply, 'No questions.'

I asked these lawyers to cross-examine a witness with a heap of questions that I had written down on a piece of paper.

'Oh, we can't ask these questions,' they replied. 'They will only embarrass the witness and the court.'

'But that's what you're supposed to do, you fuckwits,' I said. 'That's why I am paying you to prove that these witnesses, and the police, are lying.'

'Look, Mr Russell,' one of my lawyers said, 'you only have to appear in this court this one time and when it's over for you, you don't have to come back here again. My associate and I have to come back to the courts often and we have to deal with the police on a regular basis. If we embarrass them, they will make things more difficult for us in the future. If you wish to ask these questions, it is better that you ask them yourself.'

So I was left to ask my own questions in court and had to cross-examine the witness myself, through the help of the court-appointed interpreter (more about her coming up).

As my court case drew on, I realised it was up to me to defend myself.

One of the witnesses, who was a woman, took the witness stand and said, 'Yes, I know this man,' pointing at me. 'He came to my shop and brought statues and asked me to make holes in the bottom of them. He said that he wanted the holes put in them so that he could smuggle narcotics inside them to other countries around the world. He told me that he was a smuggler,' she continued.

When this was translated to me, I nearly vomited. I asked the translator to repeat what the witness had said and when my lawyers refused to cross-examine her, I stood up and said, 'I have some questions to ask the witness.'

The judge gave me the go ahead so, via the court-appointed translator, I said to the witness, 'Do you speak English?'

'No,' the witness replied.

'Well,' I said, 'I don't speak Indonesian, so how did I ask you to make holes in the statues? How did I tell you what they were for? And why would I tell you that I was a smuggler? After all, I don't even know you, not to mention that you can't speak English, and I can't speak Indonesian.'

When this was relayed to the court via the translator, the woman started to cry.

'See, see!' I yelled at the judge. 'She's a liar, she's full of bullshit, I mean lies. There is no way I could have communicated with this woman.'

The judge got pissed off and started to pound his gavel down on his bench. 'Quiet, quiet, you have caused enough trouble in this court. Look what you have done to this witness, you have upset her. You have upset her and caused her to cry with your stupid questions. I promise you this, Mr Russell, when I find you guilty you will be given the most severe sentence.'

This was a warning of what was to come.

CHAPTER 4

THE JUDGE HAD A BAD BREAKFAST . . .

He talked about death
In a very grave way

On the day of my sentence, I sat between my lawyers. One was picking his nose as usual. I watched him as he pulled a boogie from his nose and examined it, then rolled it up into a ball. He played with it for a while, rolling it between his fingers, and, I thought to myself, I wonder where he will flick it?

To my amazement, I caught him slipping his hand into his trouser pocket and then his hand came out clean. The dirty fucker, I thought, he collects snot balls in his pockets.

I know that this must sound strange but I had watched him on a number of occasions pick his nose and roll the goobies up into balls, but I always thought that he wiped them off under the table. (Christ, I felt sorry for any poor bastard who tried to pick his pockets.)

I looked over to my other lawyer, who gave me a smile and his gold tooth glinted. I thought, I couldn't trust this bastard as far as I could spit a rat, and that's what he looked like: a rat with a gold tooth. This bloke crossed his legs and I noticed for the third time that he wore no socks. My God, I thought, here I am with my life in the snotty hands of these two so-called lawyers.

I looked at my court-appointed translator and said, 'You look very sweet today. Is that a new dress?'

'Oh no,' she replied, 'it's an old one, I just haven't worn it for a long time.'

'Well, you look quite stunning in it,' I said. 'In this courtroom you look like a rose among many thorns.'

'Oh, that's very nice of you, you are such a gentleman. I really shouldn't say this, but please don't make the judge angry today. He's in a very, very bad mood and it can only help you to stay quiet,' she said.

'And how do you know that he is in a bad mood?' I asked.

'Oh, he refused to eat his breakfast. In fact, he threw the plate onto the floor before he stormed off to the court,' she replied.

'Do you know the judge well?' I asked.

'Oh yes, of course I do. He's my husband.'

That's when I knew I would be found guilty. My court-appointed translator was the judge's wife. I was fucked.

I was given a life sentence with a 50-million-rupee fine, which was equivalent to a $US50,000 fine at the time.

When the sentence was passed down, I mustered all the strength I had to ask, 'Hey judge, how long is a life sentence?'

'Until you die in prison,' he replied.

'Hey judge,' I called out, 'what about the fine. What if I die before I pay it?'

'You will pay the fine before you die, that is a court order,' he said and I was led off to the waiting van and driven back to Krobokan Prison with the judge's orders still ringing in my ears: 'You will not die before you pay your fine and you will be kept until you die in prison. That is the order of the court.'

I was stunned. I was locked up in my cell in Block H, where most of the other foreign prisoners were; dozens of black, brown and dirty white faces silently stared at me though I barely noticed them as my mind raced. I couldn't believe it – a life sentence. Well, we'll see about that, there's got to be a way out, there's just got to be a way out of this shit.

When the guards left the block, Antonio the Spaniard called out to me, 'Hey hombie, hombie, do you cry?'

'Why should I, old man,' I said.

Antonio was the oldest of all the foreigners. Everyone used to call him the Old Man, although he was only 40 years of age at the time. He had a grey streak of hair on both sides of his temples when he was first arrested, but three months after he was given a death sentence every hair on his head had turned grey.

'As long as there is life, there is hope, hombie,' he said. 'It seems we'll be together for a while yet, so pick up your guitar and play for me "The Alise".'

I sat down on my mattress, picked up my guitar and played. I played Beethoven's what I called 'For Elise'. For the next two hours I let my fingers find the strings to suit my mood.

I heard another guitar play along with me across the cell block. It was the Aussie bloke, John, who used to play in a band in Australia. We ended up playing a Tom Waites number of 'Waltzing Matilda' or 'Tom Traubert's Blues'.

If you've never heard it before, well, all I can say is that I feel sorry for you.

When I put my guitar in its place of rest and laid my head on my makeshift pillow, there was a knock on my cell wall. It was the Chook (a.k.a. James Cook).

I moved myself over to his side of the wall and I could hear his knock move up over towards the toilet window.

'What's up, Chook?' I said.

'This,' he replied. 'Put your hand into my hand.'

It was a bong.

'Have you got it?' he asked.

'Yeah, thanks, mate,' I replied as I pulled it into my cell with a pack of ciggies tied to it. When I opened the packet, there was a *mullie*, or mix, inside. I set about getting myself well and truly stoned.

The following morning I returned the bong to Chook and we had a good gum flap. The Chook was sentenced to 17 years and I had a life sentence. There was no way in hell we were going to give up and die in this shithole, so we started to make plans.

During the next few months I made an appeal to the Bunding Courts, or High Courts. My sentence was eventually reduced to 20 years and a 30-million-rupee fine, so I made another appeal to the Supreme Court.

During that period, things in Krobokan were pretty wicked.

I had spent every penny that I had on lawyers and slings, but nothing seemed to work. I had left myself totally broke but my sense of pride would not allow me to tell my family.

I was not only embarrassed, but also too ashamed to ask my family for money each month. I was under the impression that my ex-lady Sheryl would be able to support me with $100 every month. When she stopped writing to me I realised that nothing stays the same.

I had to work out a way of making money to live on in the prison. That's when I struck up a friendship with a Kiwi bloke named Kim.

Kim was a professional chef. He had just finished working at the Sydney Opera House after four and a half years and was heading to France to further his studies, when he got busted with 20 grams of hashish and was sentenced to four years imprisonment.

Kim was a reprobate and a hardcore alcoholic, but if nothing else he was a bloody good cook. It was with Kim that I struck up the *Brew* business.

Being a first-class chef, he knew how to make up home brews, so together we set about it with a vengeance. We started to buy up all of the pineapples and papayas that were available. We ordered extra sugar and started to order yeast, officially to make bread for the foreign prisoners, but of course, we ordered extra yeast.

The foreign prisoners were as happy as pigs in shit when we started to produce fresh bread and so too were the prison authorities.

The first month, we produced 50 litres of Pineapple Power (or Brum, as we nicknamed it). The boys loved it. The next month we produced 150 litres and turned a profit; from there we were cruising.

We'd sell one litre of Brum for US$1 (or whatever the buyers had to barter with that was of equal value). Any man who could drink one litre on his own made Superman look like a wimp. We were selling 100 per cent moon juice; even the bloody guards were buying it from us.

Kim, being the perfectionist that he was, insisted that we put one in every three jerry cans to the side (the more mature the juice, the more power it had, not too mention how it lessens the chances of burning your liver out).

Some of the jerry cans were 10 litres, which came in handy when we got to the point where we were making 40 to 100 litres at a time, half of which was sold outside of the prison. Kim's juice was far better than the local arak and his formula was smooth to the old tastebuds – but by Christ it sure hit you.

As you can imagine, we ended up having stashes all over the prison. The day came when the head of prison security found that half of his guards were pissed out of their heads and so too were half of the prisoners.

This turn of events occurred when Chook was caught hanging from the windows of the women's block with his prick sticking through the bars, while an Australian chick named Rita was checking it out to tell him if it tasted salty or not. They both got sprung and cell searches were conducted.

Nothing was found that day, or the next, but Kim and I couldn't rotate our jerry cans quickly enough, so for the next week we were kept on our toes.

There was another cell search and a jerry can was found in the mandi of Andrew, an Aussie bloke from Geraldton, and Scott's block. Scott was a young guy from Newcastle, NSW, Australia. Andrew took the blame, saying that it was his Vitamin C. 'Pure pineapple juice,' he said, 'I drink it every day.'

'Well, if that's the case, you can come up to the office and drink it,' the guards said, and that's just what the fucker did.

Andrew went up to the prison office every day with his mug and had his daily dose. Game bastard, I'll give him that.

After Andrew finished off the jerry can everything went quiet for a week or two, so Kim and I slipped back into business.

I had lots of problems in Krobokan Prison.

There was the time when Kim and I had our jerry cans stashed up in the roofs of the prison to mature. The weather changed and the roofs heated up, causing a majority of the jerry cans to burst.

I took the blame because at the time I was serving life, so they couldn't take any remission off my sentence. I spent a month in the Tower, which was the punishment block in Krobokan.

The reason it was called the Tower was because there was a huge water reservoir on top of the place. It must have held a million gallons and it continually leaked into the punishment cells below it. Unfortunately, the Tower became like a second home to me.

I spent two years in Krobokan, and more than one year in the Tower. In fact I spent so long there that I ended up having mushrooms growing off me. I spent monsoon seasons in the Tower, which meant that you were wet the whole time. The Tower was a cunt of a place to be when it rained.

Whenever just about anyone got caught with any Brum or were caught fighting, I took the blame. There was really nothing that they could do to me – at least officially.

CHAPTER 5

THE SECRET LADDER

After many years spent in Asia
I have learnt that in many circumstances
The most direct approach is not always
The most effective or successful

The Christmas of 1987–8 I set everything up to escape over the New Year. I knew that if I were to go over the wall by myself it would be difficult, so I enlisted the help of the Chook (James Cook) and the Don (Guiseppe Taranto). The Don was serving 12 years for selling heroin to an undercover policeman in Kuta.

The plot was pretty straightforward: get over the wall and fuck off. I say this to make a long story short. Get over the wall and fuck off sounds easy, but it wasn't.

First we needed a way out of the country, passports, tickets and disguises and once those were arranged we had to get out of the prison without being detected. I set my mind to working out all of these finer points.

Arranging the passports for the Chook and the Don was quite easy and once the passports were in my hands, the Don arranged for a camera. I was in charge of the make-over. It's amazing what a good haircut and close shave can achieve – when I finished with the Don, he looked like a new man.

The Chook was another matter. I got him to shave the top of his head (he was thinning anyway) and stuffed some cotton wool up his nose and in his cheeks, hoping to fatten the skinny fucker up a bit. I splashed some Clearasil under his eyes to cover his dark circles (he looked like a fucking endangered species before the Clearasil), which gave him a younger appearance.

When I had the Chook looking as good as I was going to get him, I flashed away with the camera.

The photos turned out great and once the passports were doctored up the next job was getting out of that cesspit, and that wasn't all that hard.

The best thing to use to get over a wall is a ladder and in Krobokan one could be found. The guards there were as greedy as newborn calves – if they found a tit to milk they stuck to it.

I was still working in the kitchen with Kim, cooking the food for the foreigners, so it gave me the chance to front the head of security, a Mr Susanta. I asked him for permission to breed rabbits so that the prisoners could have extra meat in their diets. The prison only supplied 65 grams of meat twice a week to each of the prisoners and that meat was pretty suspect. At first the head of security refused, but when I said 'Oh, sir, that's a shame, I'm sure your wife would have loved to cook a couple of rabbits every month for you.'

'Ah, what do you mean?' he asked.

'I was intending on going 50/50 with you, sir, you know, once they're breeding. Half for you and half for me and the boys. Didn't I mention that before?'

'Oh well, in that case,' he said, 'I don't want to disappoint you boys. Yes, of course you can have some rabbits. Yes, that's a good idea. Where do you propose to keep them?'

'Well, I was thinking that we could build a small run for them just outside my cell, sir, and that way I can keep an eye on them, just in case any of the cats try to steal any of the babies when they are born. You know what the cats are like here, sir. They ate all of Made's [pronounced *Mar-day*] pigeons last week,' I said.

'Yes, yes, I heard about that. Very well, you have my permission to breed your rabbits. How many do you intend to start with?' he asked.

'Well, I was thinking of about six females and one male, if that's OK, sir,' I replied. 'I'll also need your permission to buy some cement wire and a little wood, if that's alright with you.'

'Yes, yes anything you need. Just give the money to Mr Tantra and he will buy it for you,' he said.

An hour later, Mr Tantra was on his way to do the shopping with a pocket full of rupees.

The rabbit cage was three metres long and a little over one metre wide; the sides were built of stone and cement, except for the front, which was of chicken wire. The roof was made of thatched grass, woven to two long pieces of three-by-three-inch wooden poles. The roof was attached to catches in the front of the cage so that it could be swung upwards in order to clean the cage.

In all honesty the whole thing looked pretty innocent – well, kind of innocent considering the roof of the cage was our secret ladder. Not your common, conventional, horizontal step-ladder, but a ladder nevertheless Made with crossed wooden sections so we could climb up it. It was camouflaged with wire and thatched grass.

On the night we planned to escape we could easily unhook it completely off the rabbit cage and run, lean it up against the wall, scarper up, then once on top, kick the ladder back, letting it fall back inside the prison.

Laying flat, covered in thatched grass, the makeshift ladder would easily blend in with the surrounding grass on the ground inside the prison compound, making it harder for the guards to see it after we were gone – giving us more time to get away.

Bloody brilliant, hey!

A couple of foreign prisoners jerried on to it straight away – Kim for one and Antonio for another.

On the morning just before the release of an Aussie bloke named Max, I had just finished cleaning out the rabbit cage with the Chook when Kim turned up. He poked a few scraps of food into the cage and when he stood up he looked at the Chook and me, then back at the cage.

'If I didn't know better,' he said, with a grin on his dial, 'I'd swear you were breeding racing rabbits – nice long cage, give the little bastards room to run when they get the urge, hey! If there is anything I can do to help you blokes, let me know and the best of luck to you,' he said and off he went to the kitchen.

'The fucker knows,' the Chook said, pissed off, looking like a bald gnome with a bad attitude.

'He knows nothing,' I said. 'He's guessing but he's not a total fuckwit, you've got to give him that.'

'Yeah, well he's guessing pretty good, the prick. What do you think?' Chook said.

'I'm thinking about that roof,' I said, as I nodded towards the rabbit cage. 'How strong is it?'

'A fucking elephant could walk up it,' the Chook replied.

'Yeah well, when the time comes, we go up it one at a time, just to play it safe, fair enough!' I said.

'Mate, don't you have any faith? I told you I worked as a carpenter once,' the Chook said.

'Yeah, for two weeks and you got the arse,' I replied, and headed off to join Kim in the kitchen.

When I got there Kim was as busy as a one-armed Bangkok taxi driver with crabs in peak hour. We were going to have a going-away party for Max and Kim was running around giving orders here and there with a mug of pineapple juice in his hand.

The kitchen guards turned a blind eye to our brews because they were the ones who were selling it outside.

When things settled down a bit, Kim came over to the table where I was working some dough for the bread and said, 'Here, have a drink. It's my birthday today and I am going to get faced. This brew is nearly eight weeks old and I've been keeping it for today. Come on, let's get legless together.'

'Well, if that's the case,' I said, as I picked up the mug, 'happy birthday, Sunshine.' We started to get drunk.

Max joined us in the kitchen and as the day drew on we ended up in his cell, along with about 20 other foreigners, all getting smashed on the brew.

A couple of the more cool guards joined us and as the time progressed, half the prisoners ended up as drunk as skunks.

Max pulled out half of his going-home money and brought up every litre of brew that we had stashed, some of which was less than one week old, but at the time no one seemed to care – this was a party!

Kim did the dance of the flaming arseholes. He stuck a piece of long newspaper up his arse, got someone to light it and started to do the Cha Cha with Antonio the Spaniard.

Sam passed out face first into a hot steaming plate of rice and when he came to he had thousands of little red spots on his face, not to mention quite a few blisters also, making him look like he had the chicken pox . . . or something worse.

Phillipe the Frenchie had a piss fight with another French bloke named Lolos. They were running around the block with their pricks in their hands trying to piss on each other.

One of the newer foreign prisoners, a Maori from New Zealand, who had arms as thick as my thighs, was stamping around in his underpants, doing the Haka, or Maori war dance, with his tongue sticking out about two feet from his face. He looked like he was choking on an elephant's liver.

The Chook was kicking the shit out of an Indonesian prisoner called Horse Face for stealing his mirror.

Serge, another French bloke, was spitting all the saliva that his gob could muster at another guy for stealing his slope boyfriend. 'Nazi, Nazi, Nazi, you don't love him, it's just lust, you Nazi, Nazi, Nazi,' he screamed.

By this time we had worked out that the guy was either German or Austrian.

'Viva La France,' Baba, who was another Frenchman, cried out as he vomited over his fellow countryman, which to everyone's approval stopped Serge's bitch fight.

All in all, it was a pretty good going-away party for Max. When the party was broken up by the change of the guards we were all locked up in our cells at five in the afternoon.

I crashed out straight away, but at 7.00 p.m. the guards came to visit. I was still a bit tipsy when they opened my cell. The guard in charge of the cell search was a bloke named Darma, a 100 per cent total prick.

The guards searched my cell and found no knives or contraband.

'You had a good party today, you and your pig friends, didn't you? But only one of your friends is going home and it's not you. You will die in this prison, you will never go home,' he said and slapped me across the face. 'You will always be here at least for the next 20 years and when your hair is grey I will watch you crawl out of my country a broken man.' He slapped me again in the face.

On the second hit I totally lost my temper and grabbed him by the shirt with both hands, pulled him towards me and, lifting up my right knee, I smashed it into his stomach. When he bent forward, I slipped back then grabbed his head. I pulled it towards mine, head-butting him in the face and smashing his nose. I released him and let him fall to the floor, then kicked down on the kneecap of a guard who was standing to the right of me. I rushed over him, towards the door of my cell and out. I found myself in the middle of the cell block where all the other prisoners could see me.

As the guards surrounded me, all I could see was red.

'Behind you Russ, get the cunt,' I heard the Chook yell out and, as I turned, a guard was swinging at me with his baton. I side-stepped him and as he rushed passed I pulled his arm up and down and he did a complete flip.

It really must have been pretty to watch, because all of the prisoners started to yell and scream.

I could hear Antonio yell out, 'Bravo, bravo, bravo.'

The Frenchies were screaming, '*Magnifique, magnifique.*'

But the last words I heard were those of the Chook yelling out, 'Behind you, behind you, you fuckwit, you cunts,' and then *bang*, the lights were turned off.

When I woke up I was in the Tower. Christ, I thought, what the fuck happened? As my mind started to clear, I began thinking about the most ridiculous things. Have the horses been fed? Did my servants wax my boots? Have the rabbits had babies? Why can't I breathe properly?

My mind was reeling in a thousand different directions, until I heard a familiar voice call out, 'Russ, Russ. Hey, Russell, Russell, are you OK?'

It was Kim and he was in the cell of the Tower that was opposite mine. My name isn't Russell, my name is Chris. Christopher, that's right, now I remember. I am in prison and here my name is Russell. Get your shit together, I started to tell myself, get it together.

'Russ, Russ, Russell, mate, are you OK?' Kim called out to me again.

'Yeah,' I replied, 'I'm sweet, but what the fuck happened?'

'You tried to fight the fuckers, that's what happened and they nearly killed you, you stupid fuck,' he said.

'Yeah and you nearly killed Darma the Shit Cloth. I could see him being carried out from my window,' said Lolos the Frog.

'What happened in your block, it sure must have been good. Everybody was yelling and screaming. What happened?' Lolos asked.

'I am not too sure, it all went down too fast, but how come you two blokes are in here?' I asked.

'They did a cell search and I had a jerry can in my cell,' Kim said. 'And Lolos was still pretty fucked up when they came in. As soon as they opened his cell to search it he ran out and over to Phillipe's cell, and started to piss on Phillipe as he stood at the cell door yelling out, "Touché, touché", the fuckwit.'

'Christ, I can hardly breathe,' I said.

'It's a wonder you can breathe at all,' Lolos said. 'Dildo was jumping on you like a bed bug, but Tantra pulled them all off you and took their keys so they couldn't come back and get you. Good man that, good man.'

'Yeah,' I tried to say, then realised how sore my throat was, not to mention my chest.

That morning I woke up hurting. I could only breathe in short gasps and my throat and neck were killing me.

The guards came into the Tower at about 7.00 a.m. and took Kim to the KPLP office, which is the office for prison security.

After Kim was taken away, Lolos called out to me, saying, 'They're going to give Kim a good beating. I just heard Dildo talking to the other guards.' Lolos had spent over six years on Bali and was married to a local girl so could speak fluent Indonesian and Balinese.

'Hey, Lolos,' I said, 'Dildo worked last night. He should have gone home by now, along with all the other niggers on the shift.'

'Half of them didn't want to go home,' Lolos replied. 'They wanted to stick around with the morning shift so that they can help beat the fuck out of us.'

The news didn't help to start my day well. Dildo was one of the cruellest of the guards. His real name was Wedodo, but he was such a prick we nicknamed him Dildo, the plastic prick.

When I managed to get myself off the ground I staggered over to the cell door, which was made out of square steel bars about two inches thick and two inches wide. The whole door was crossed with these two-by-two steel bars, which created gaps big enough to stick your head through.

I pushed my head through to check out the other cells in the Tower. Counting the one that I was in, there were nine cells in the punishment block.

I could see Lolos's head sticking out from his cell door looking at me. With his huge hooked nose and protruding front jaw, he looked like a real-life Punch and Judy doll with the same squarky attitudes. With his arms lazily swinging either side of his head through the bars, you would think he was a puppet. Seeing my head poking through brought an instant smile to Lolos's blank face.

'Ah, good morning, sir. What would you like? The Continental Breakfast or the American? We can grind it up into a nice tasty fine paste so that you can suck it through a straw and not upset those Zeppelin lips of yours,' he said, still smiling.

What the fuck are you raving on about, I thought. Then I felt my mouth. I was shocked. My bottom lip felt like a bloody Dunlop bicycle tube without the tyre to protect it, fully pumped up and ready to explode. The more I fondled it, the more I was amazed. I must have had the biggest fat lip in the world! What really pissed me off were the loose teeth. The bastards, I thought, they nearly kicked out my bloody teeth.

'Hey, Los,' I said. 'How do I look?'

'Well, my friend,' he replied, 'if my dog dragged you in from the street, I'd kick its arse. But don't worry too much about your looks now, it's when you come back from the office that you should worry. Hero is with them and so is your mate Darma.'

'Shit,' I moaned, 'that's all I need.'

Hero was another guard who was a basher, but he only bashed prisoners when they were handcuffed and on the floor – that's how he got his name Hero. He was a wimp, but a very cruel and vicious wimp if ever there was one.

'Thanks for the good news, Los. I think I'll give the breakfast a miss this morning, but you can tell the chambermaid to change the sheets,' I said.

'Ah, so the gentleman had a lady in last night, did he?' Lolos said, still smiling.

'No, you long-nosed frog. If I didn't shit myself last night, I am sure to any minute now. That brew that we drank yesterday is still working, and I am in desperate need of a crap. I can taste it in the back of my throat,' I said.

'Then you can forget that tongue kiss I promised you, blubber lips,' Lolos threw in.

I pulled my head in and started looking for a place in my cell to have a shit. In the Tower there were no functioning toilets. You had to shit into plastic bags, if you could get your hands on one, or just shit on the floor, which was definitely something to be avoided. After all, you had to sleep and live on the floor and I didn't know how long I'd be held in the Tower this time. So I had to hold back on having a crap, which was really killing me because the yeast in the brew that I had been drinking the day before was still percolating in my guts.

I decided to try and hang in and wait until I could get someone to sneak me in some plastic bags.

Have you ever tried to hold back a shit to the point that you could taste it in the back of your throat? If not, try it sometime, it's good fun . . .

Two hours later, the guards came for me. They tried to handcuff me, but I refused, saying, 'If this is only going to be a report to Mr Susanta (the KPLP head), then there is no need for handcuffs. I won't give any trouble, but I won't leave this cell in handcuffs.'

I wedged myself against the corner of the cell expecting the worst when Mr Tantra, the guard who had taken the key from my cell the night before, came in. He pushed the other guards aside and said, 'It's all right, Russell, come with me into the office.'

As I was led into the KPLP office from the Tower I got a quick glimpse of the Chook and Andrew cutting grass just outside the entrance of the prison offices. Both using sickles, they laboured away in the early morning sun. The sweat dripped off their well-tanned, half-naked, and malnourished bodies.

The Chook gave me a knowing nod and when our eyes met a million words were spoken. The Chook knew that I was being taken in for a beating and very likely one that could, or would, cripple me. He looked at me and then down at his sickle. I gave him a subtle shake of my head as if to say, 'no, mate, stay where you are'. There, I thought to myself, is a very solid mate.

As I was marched into the office of the prison security section, Mr

Tantra was ordered to go away. I stood there for what seemed ages but was probably no more than half an hour, until I was pushed into another office.

The first thing I saw was Kim, his face covered in blood. As he looked up at me, he held up his hand. I could see that the fingers on his right hand were sticking out at all awkward angles. 'They've broken my fucking fingers,' he said as he coughed and spat out a tooth. He coughed again into his left hand catching another tooth, and I realised that the guards had smashed out at least three or four, if not more, of his teeth.

When he stopped coughing he looked up at me again from the chair where they had him sitting and started to cry. 'I am only here for fucking dope, fucking dope. I am just a fucking cook and they've broken my fucking fingers. Where the fuck is justice in this fucking place? I am just a fucking cook.'

He kept on crying as he looked down at the teeth in his hand.

The guards started to move in on me. There were about ten of them. Some were holding batons in their hands, some were holding clusters of keys on iron rings and still others were holding big Chinese locks (the ones that were used to lock up the cells and prison blocks) – they were huge. These bastard guards had told me on a number of occasions that they could kill me in Krobokan Prison and no one would question it. Deaths in Indonesian prisons are a common occurrence – just ask the Indonesian Government.

I knew that I was in for a hiding, the hiding of my life, and very possibly death.

I knew that there was no way that I could fight them all and win, not in the physical sense, but then again there's more than one way to kill a cat. Apart from stuffing 10 kilograms of hot butter up its arse . . . and that's just how I felt with what I had in my stomach at the time.

As the guards closed in on me, I screamed out, 'Stop! Stop! Look! Look!' which caused them to pause for a moment. I held up my arms to yell out something or other when suddenly the stress of it all caused me to actually shit myself.

I was wearing a pair of Bombay bloomers, which are a pair of very loose-fitting baggy short pants, and the yeast-assisted shit just poured from my bum all over the office floor.

The guards all looked at me in amazement and then down at the huge pile of shit that had just dropped out of me.

'Now just look at what you've done,' I said, as I bent down and picked up two handfuls of it. 'Look, look, look at this,' I yelled, as I stood up and held out two handfuls of shit to the guards. They just stood there, their eyes expanding like small saucers, then slowly they started to back off.

I got another cramp in my stomach and again shat myself. I watched as the pile of shit beneath me started to grow. The guards started to back off even more, and that's when I began to throw it at them.

If I live to be 1,000 years old, I'll never forget that day. When I started to throw my shit at them they all took off in a dozen different directions, dropping their batons, chains, key rings and locks.

As Dildo pulled Hero back by the shirt so as to get out of the office door first, Hero slipped and fell to the ground. The lucky prick. The handful of shit that I had thrown at him flew over the top of his falling body and hit Dildo on the back of the head. As it splashed through his hair, he screamed as though hit by a bullet. He fell against the wall with both his hands clasped to the back of his head. In an award-winning drama-queen way, he spun around and looked at me in total shock, then pulled his hands away from the back of his head. He looked at the shit that was all over his hands and started to dry retch.

That's when I had a clear shot at him and the next fistful of shit hit him fair square in the gob. Beautiful it was, fucking beautiful. I literally made him eat shit. Darma picked this moment to walk into the office, and to my total surprise his nose was a match for my lips – big, fat and sore. You could say that he walked into the office just as the shit hit the fan – straight into a flying turd.

As he already hated my guts, having my shit smeared across his rough head sent him into a complete frenzy. He picked up a baton and rushed over towards me, but before reaching me, Hero stood up in a half crouch and Darma went face first over the top of him landing at my feet.

By this time the office was almost totally empty. Hero had managed to get out of the place along with most of his mates. The only people left in the office were Kim, who was in total shock but smiling, a guard named Weassa, who was hiding behind a desk, and Darma, who was at my feet . . . a bad place to be!

I looked down at him and as he lifted his head I said, 'You once promised to kill me, that wasn't nice, Mr Darma,' and I kicked up with all I had into his upturned face – crack, crunch. Music to my ears! I was truly under the belief that he was dead, and it didn't seem to bother me in the slightest (which is scary to say the least). I was seriously losing the plot.

I started to pick up shit and cover all the typewriters in the office with it – I really did flip out. I walked over to Kim and said, 'Well mate, that's how it's done,' and then I shat myself again.

Then I noticed Weassa hiding behind the desk. I pointed at him and said, 'I can see you,' and leapt over the desk and grabbed the little prick by the hair, pulled him to his feet and said, 'Are you scared of me?'

He nodded without saying a word. I grabbed him by the ears, gave him a kiss on the lips and threw him over the desk. As he slipped on the shit-covered floor I jumped over the desk again and landed in front of him, helping him back up onto his feet.

'It's OK, I love you, I won't hurt you. I love you all,' I said as I guided him out the office door. Kim was totally stunned.

When I returned to Kim, he said, 'I only came to Bali for a holiday, God help me, I'm going mad, I only came here for a fucking holiday. I'm a cook, I'm just a fucking cook.' He started crying again. Then Mr Susanta came in with the gun-toting prison director.

The laws of the prisons in Indonesia stipulate that when guns are used on prisoners, the prison director must be informed first, if possible, hence the prison director came in with his gun. If there was any shooting to do, he wanted to do it.

I don't think he was expecting to see shit everywhere and two foreign prisoners, whose faces were covered with blood and shit, both crouched on chairs, one crying, 'I'm a cook, I'm just a fucking cook.'

I looked up at the prison director and Chief Susanta and said, 'He just wants to cook, but I really needed to go to the toilet.' I gave Kim a cuddle. 'Isn't that right?' Kim started to cry more.

All this shit and blood was too much for the director and he ordered the guards to take us back to the Tower. As we were marched back to the cells I caught sight of the Chook, still cutting grass. He lifted his head, gave me a smile and started to laugh.

It was nearly three days before the other foreign prisoners could pass by our cell and the first bloke to visit me was the Chook.

Hysterically he said, 'By Christ mate, you did the most radical of the fucking radical things back in that KPLP office. When we saw the guards all bolting out of the office, Andrew and I didn't know what to think. I was so geared up I was going to run in there and justify my 17-year sentence with that fucking sickle and start chopping at a couple of the rice suckers, but when we found out that you had thrown shit on them, I nearly pissed myself laughing. Mate, all I can say is that I wish I had met you in Sydney, we would have torn the place apart.'

'The cunt is bent,' said Kim from the opposite cell. 'He gave Weassa a fucking kiss on the lips, then threw the prick over the fucking table. If that's not mad, I don't know what is!'

'Magnifique, magnifique,' cried Lolos from another cell.

'That must have really fucked up his head. Did you really kiss the cunt?' Chook asked.

'Sure did,' I replied. 'I saw the director and Susanta coming through the office windows so I thought I'd blow them out.'

'Christ, radical is not the word for you,' the Chook said, then dropping his voice he added, 'but you do realise that the racing rabbits have to be put off now, until you get out of the Tower?'

'Yeah,' I said. 'I am sorry about that, but then again, we're supposed to go at Christmas, during the Monsoon, and by that time all this shit will be forgotten.'

'Yeah, that is if your ribs are healed. How are the old bones anyway?' the Chook said.

'They hurt like shit, mate. I need to see a doctor. It feels as if they're pushing into my lungs. Do me a favour and try to get me a plaster or bandage to wrap around the bludgers,' I said.

'Will do,' the Chook said.

The guards came into the Tower and when they saw the Chook, they questioned why he was there.

'Just bringing in their food, sir,' Chook replied as he scampered off in the opposite direction.

The next day my chest was hurting more then ever, not to mention my lip, jaw, face and everything else below the neck. My broken ribs and other injuries made it hard to even talk, let alone get off the cane mat on the floor of the punishment block. I couldn't keep anything down, though I still had the shits and I kept vomiting up bile with odd bits of blood in it. So I stopped eating. The first few days were quite hard because I suffered some pretty savage hunger pains, but they were nothing compared to when I had to relieve myself into the plastic bags the foreign prisoners sent in with my food.

After the fourth day of not eating, I didn't get off the cane mat on the floor. I didn't move when the food was brought into my cell, or should I say pushed between the bars of the Tower, and I didn't need to relieve my bowels any more.

I had gone nearly a week without food when Guiseppe the Italian prisoner realised that I hadn't been eating for days. 'Why you no eat?' he asked.

'Because I don't eat shit,' I replied weakly.

'I don't feed you shit,' he said, looking saddened.

'I know that, mate,' I answered, 'but the prison feeds us shit. I worked in the kitchen, remember, I know what the prison gives us, and it's shit. They give us foreigners the food that they can't sell in the market, they give us meat that dogs outside wouldn't eat, they give us *shit* and, now that my ribs are broken, I don't need their shit. You and the others can eat it, I won't,' I said.

'What you mean by that?' he asked.

'Surely you know, Guiseppe, the prison is ripping off our food. The bastards are so corrupt they think that we can live on water. I am not hungry, mate. I don't want to eat shit any more,' I said.

'Hey, you talk shit, we got the rabbits, porca Madonna, where your face? We gotta the rabbits, we can go, you get strong. Better you eat mate, and you, me, and Chook, we can go easy. The cage, she's a ready, so better you eat, getta the strong and we can all fuck off, OK!' Guiseppe said pleadingly.

'Yeah, yeah, we'll fuck off OK,' I said as I slipped into a deep sleep, a sleep of soft sand beneath me, a sleep where I could hear the waves on the beach of Hickidua, splashing on the shore. Where I could feel the warm sunshine beating down on my body. Where the musical laughter of my wife and kids washed away the pain, the hunger, the cold and the loneliness.

I was slipping into the sleep of a man who had gone seven days without food.

As a boy my father taught me how to fight – boxing and judo. I remember clearly one day, before a lesson had started, he picked up my small hands and folded them up into tiny fists then squeezing them gently he said, 'These are your weapons, son, use them when you have to, but always remember, they are only extensions of your real strength. Your true strength is inside you, it is in every breath you breathe.'

As I lay back on the cane mat in the prison in Bali with my broken ribs and empty belly, I did what very few Western men could do. I let my mind go to places where only dreams are, as my body repaired itself. I let my mind go to the highest mountains of the Himalayas where I could look upon the world and part the clouds with a wave of my hand.

I let my thoughts go back to a Chinese junk sailing the South China Sea, where I could tell the clouds or rain to go this way or that.

As the days passed without food in my stomach I began to feel stronger, on a different level.

I could see people on a war-torn wharf in Da Nang screaming for freedom, food and peace, as bombs were thrown at them. I could redirect those missiles of death into the sea and no one would suffer the pain or anguish that each projectile carried with it.

The longer I went without food, it seemed to me at the time, the better I could make the world – or should I say, re-make it.

The word had gotten out via Guiseppe and Chook that I was on a hunger strike because of the prison food, and the prison conditions. I was transferred to Block C, the Communist block in Krobokan, but that didn't stop all the other foreign prisoners joining me on a hunger strike for better food, conditions and treatment. My fast went on for 23 days, after which time the embassies of a dozen different countries came to the prison in Bali. With the intervention of so many foreign embassies, consulates and diplomatic missions the Indonesian Prisons Department graciously increased our food ration by $US0.25 a day.

Once the food and conditions were improved, the hunger strike was called off. However, I was still kept in the Communist block.

The day after the hunger strike ended, the Don and Lolos were moved into C block with me.

You know it's quite amazing how strong and solid some people can be when they're in a hard spot.

Have you been there?

My real friends showed their colours while I was in C Block, and they weren't all Australians, as one may expect. There were two Kiwis, a Spaniard, a Dutch bloke named August and a frog dog named Phillipe. They, of all the foreigners in Krobokan Prison, showed enough courage to risk coming to see me after the shit hit the fan – literally!

The only Aussies that came to see me were John, from Byron Bay, and

Andrew. They only passed by my cell to say 'G'day', then split as quickly as they came.

August the Dutchie, Antonio the Spaniard, Phillipe the Frenchie, Kim and David the two Kiwis, all stopped long enough to slip me food or cigarettes, not to mention keep me informed of any prison news. They were solid people.

The only other prisoner in C block with us was a little old Commie bloke named Pak Puji who was once a member of the PKI, which was the Communist Party of Indonesia before President Soeharto and his cronies wiped out over a million of them in the mid 1960s.

Pak Puji was glad to have our company. He was a very lonely old man who had spent over 23 years in prison. Only the year before, two of his mates, who he had spent all those 23 years with, had been taken out and executed by firing squad.

Pak Puji was a top bloke who spoke English, Dutch, Chinese and half-a-dozen local Indonesian languages. He was only a small man and always spoke very softly and very clearly in whatever language he would be using. For a man in his mid 60s he worked like a man who was in his mid 40s, but I put that down to his Chinese blood.

August the Dutch prisoner said that Pak Puji spoke better Dutch than he did and his English was so deceptive that you couldn't place where he had learnt it. He didn't have any accent, if you know what I mean. He didn't sound like an Asian when he spoke and his English was probably 100 per cent better than 50 per cent of the Aussies and Kiwis.

Although he was a very small man, his mere presence commanded respect and even the guards called him Pak, which means Mr or Sir in Indonesian.

Pak Puji was also the prison's unofficial doctor, and he was pretty good at it. During the period that I was alone in Block C fasting with broken ribs, the guards would let him into my cell to administer his needles.

He was the Master of Acupuncture and, while my ribs were repairing, he would stick me full of needles and the pain would go away. It was old Pak

Puji who wrapped up my chest and told me that two of my ribs were broken and that three others had been cracked.

'But the break is outwards,' he said. 'So at least they won't puncture your lungs, although they will be very painful.'

While on the hunger strike he would make up concoctions of God knew what and insist that I drink them, which I did. Some of them were quite tasty and some of them nearly made me spew.

One time he came in with what looked like a mug of mud and said, 'Please, drink this, Mr Russell. I know that it does not look very appetising, and probably smells worse, but you have an infection in your blood. See this red line?' He pointed to a red line that was running up my leg. 'You have blood poisoning or what is known in the West as tetanus. This will help kill the bacterium.'

I knew what tetanus was and I also knew that lock-jaw was not a nice way to go, so I started to drink from the mug that he gave me. It tasted rotten and after drinking half the mug I paused to run my tongue around my mouth.

Whatever I was drinking was gritty; bits and pieces of whatever it was were sticking between my teeth. I shook my head and said, 'What's it made of, Mr Puji? It tastes like a crunched up thong, with a dash of horse shit in it.'

'Well, I don't have your culinary experience,' he said with a smile, 'but finish the cup and we'll discuss the highlights of your gourmet adventures later.'

I polished off the rest of the mug and for the following week all the other mugs of this foul-tasting gear that he gave to me, and I watched as the red line on my leg receded; the open weeping scabs on my body closed up and healed as Pak Puji administered his traditional Chinese medicine to me.

As I've said, he was a top bloke and he had his own sense of humour, even if it was drier than a constipated camel's arsehole.

Lolos, the Don and I spent nearly five months in Block C. While we were there Lolos made himself a cricket omelette and ended up with a bad dose of the shits. Crickets have a way of hiding under rocks, or in drainpipes, especially sewerage drainpipes, and then happily cricketing away.

Lolos had gathered as many crickets as he could find, shoving them into one of the plastic bags we had collected. He then filled the bag with hot water, killing them all. This is the quickest way of killing crickets, or cockroaches if that's what you favour. When a cricket is doused in hot water it loses control of its bowels, leaving you with a fairly clean meal (well, on most occasions). But you should always remember to give them a second wash – Lolos was just too slack and didn't bother. Once they were dead, he picked the crickets out of the bag, mixed them in with an egg, then fried them up with some *Lombok Kucil* (small chilli peppers) and ate them.

It wasn't long before Lolos was as sick as a dog, and shitting through the eye of a needle. Pak Puji made him up one of his special 'bum blocker brews' and gave it to Lolos to drink. The Don turned up, looked at the mystery mix and said, 'Porca Dia, you no going to drink that are you?'

'Sure I am, it's good traditional medicine,' Lolos said, wiggling his comical-looking head.

'But what is that shit and why does it have legs?' Don questioned.

'Eye of newt, wing of bat,' I said to the Don, 'with just a sprinkle of dried frog's skin.'

'Don't forget the fried spiders,' said Old Pak Puji.

'What are the fried spiders for?' Lolos asked, mock-seriously, pushing his nose into the conversation with a slight shake to his head.

'To give it some body,' said Pak Puji with a straight face, 'and to add to the flavour.'

'Yummy,' Los replied as he skolled the mug.

'Jesus Kristus,' said the Don, totally horror struck, and as he bolted out of the cell, Lolos and I cracked up. Pak Puji sat there with a blank look on his face.

'I liked the bit about the fried spiders to give it body and add to the flavour,' I said, 'that really blew the Don away. He really believes you threw spiders in that medicine.'

'Yeah, he really believed you,' said Lolos, still laughing.

'But there was,' Pak Puji said, and walked out of the cell leaving Lolos and me just staring at each other, not knowing whether to believe him or not.

That was the type of person old Pak Puji was. He always got the last laugh.

CHAPTER 6

THE GRADUATES OF MURPHY'S LAW

May you live in interesting times
(An old Chinese curse)

At the end of 1987, Lolos was released and the Don and I were returned to D Block. We both had to give the KPLP boss Susanta a back-hand (also known as a bribe).

I managed to get back my old cell, with the rabbit cage outside, and the Don was to be my cell mate, with the Chook on his own in the cell next to ours. We all played it cool and kept out of trouble as best we could, as we put our plans of escape into action.

After yet another bribe to Susanta I got back my job in the kitchen with Kim and prison life returned to some semblance of normality.

As Christmas drew near, our escape plan was refined. Gary, a friend of mine, turned up with copies of the most recent exit and entry stamps of Bali's international airport along with blank disembarkation forms.

We planned to escape during the evening of 26 December: Boxing Day night.

The week before we were set to go, the Don and I pretended to have an argument. The Don had already slipped Susanta a back-hand saying that he couldn't stay in the same cell with me because I had this strange fetish of slipping bags of shit under his pillow. With my reputation from the shit fight in the prison office, the Don managed quite easily to get moved into Musaki's (one of the Japanese prisoners) cell.

Part of the plan was that the Chook and I would slip out of our cells and cut across the block into the Don's cell. We couldn't piss off from the Chook's cell or the one I was in because we were in a corner of the prison block that could be seen from either the prison office or from where the bell was.

The bell was a big bloody brass prick of a thing. The guards in the front of the prison, where the offices were situated, would come out every two hours and bang on this bell to keep the guards in the seven wall tower posts awake. Well that was the theory, but in fact this was all bullshit, because the guards in the towers did their own thing at night: drinking, gambling, fornicating, or just getting some shut-eye.

On the night of the 26 December I ordered 100 Nasi Padang, which is basically a bag of rice with a decent-sized piece of meat inside cooked in a curry-style sauce. When the takeaway packs of rice, or Nasi Bunkus, arrived they were delivered to my cell through the back window bars.

Once the guard who had delivered them pissed off, I started to open them in lots of 10 and load them up with Lexotan sleeping pills, 12 mg to every pack.

As I was loading them up, trying to keep one eye on the windows and the other on the job, a guard popped his head up to my cell window. 'What are you doing Russell?' he said. It must have been pretty obvious, even to a *blind* man, what I was doing, but then again, most Indonesian prison guards are classified as gifted if they have an IQ of ten.

'Oh, umm, I'm picking out the meat, Pak,' I said. 'After all, I did buy these Nasi Bunkus, Pak, and there's lots of meat in them. Here.' I pushed one of the unloaded ones up to the window.

'Try this,' I said, and the greedy prick grabbed it and started to stuff his face. As he did so I repacked the loaded Nasi Padangs, which were still lying opened on my cell floor. When I had finished I put them to the side and pulled out ten packs, which were still unlaced with sleeping pills.

'Hey Pak,' I said to the guard, 'can you take these over to Block F and give them to Kim and tell him they're from Russell – and say Merry Christmas. Oh, and here's 5,000 rupee for you, sir. Merry Christmas.' As I said, the guards were definitely not over-burdened with brains.

His eyes lit up, 5,000 rupee was the equivalent of $US5. He was stoked as he went off to Kim's block with the bags of rice.

I then loaded up ten more Nasi Padangs, but this time I kept my ears peeled for the sound of footsteps outside my cell.

The week before, Chook and a couple of local prisoners helped me lay gravel, small rocks and whatnot that we found around the prison, outside my cell, so I could hear any of the bastards if they walked passed at night.

I was starting to get pissed off with myself though. Somehow I must have left patches in the path, which meant I'd missed the footsteps of this particular guard as he walked up to my cell. On his return I was waiting.

'Here, Pak,' I said, as I thrust another ten bags of Nasi Padang at him through the barred window. 'Can you give these to John in Block G.' Off he went with the next load of pill-less Nasi Padangs.

Soon after the guard had gone about those other deliveries, the Chook started to bash on my wall. 'What the fuck are you doing?' he asked. 'Where's the fucking Nasi Bunkus for all the slopes in this block?'

'I'm dressing them up, baldy,' I replied, 'and I've got a fucking homing pigeon guard that keeps returning to my window. Here, try this. Can you taste anything in this Nasi Padang?' I slipped him a trial bag of rice.

I watched him open it, and as he stuck his fingers into the rice and meat sauce, his face screwed up as if he had just tasted shit. 'Fucking horrible, can't taste a thing,' he said.

Just then I heard the gravel crunching outside. I zipped back to the window just in time to catch the guard, but this time he was with one of his mates.

'Hey,' the guard said, 'have you got a Nasi for my friend? He hasn't had anything to eat yet tonight.'

'Nasi,' I replied, 'of course I've got a Nasi for your mate. Here,' and I slipped him one of the doctored suckers.

'Hey look, can you and your mate drop five Nasi Padangs off to Andrew the fisherman in Block E and five more off to Phillipe the Frenchman in Block H, and when you get back I'll have a Christmas present for you,' I said. With this, both the guards were off.

I managed to load up the rest of the Nasi Padangs with sleepers while they were gone. When the guards returned I gave them another 5,000 rupee, or $US5, with 30 packs of Nasi Padangs, each loaded up with 12 mg of Lexotans, telling them to share them around with their mates. The rest I passed around to all the local prisoners in my block and within two hours the whole prison was like a morgue.

It was time.

I pulled out the cut-off bar that was in the corner of my cell, which led into our block (I had cut this out weeks before and superglued it back on), then headed for Musaki's cell. The Don had cut away the bars of his cell to let me and the Chook in.

This cell faced the outside prison wall and it was in total darkness – perfect for our escape.

Once outside, all we had to do was drop down into the storm drain as far as the rabbit cage, unclip the roof, pull it down into the storm drain, run back along the drain up to the wall, lean the roof of the rabbit cage up against the wall of the prison, climb up the roof-cum-ladder, kick the ladder back, lower ourselves down as far as we could with our hands on the other side, then jump into the rice paddies that ran alongside the walls of the prison. Simple . . . except for one thing.

The prison director chose that night to pull a spot check on the guards, and when he found that half of them were asleep and the other half were preparing to lay down, he went apeshit.

He set off alarms and bells that I didn't even know the prison had, nor I am sure, did most of the guards. He picked a block at random to do a cell search and guess which block it was? That's right, yours fucking truly!

Man, oh man, now we're in the shit, I thought to myself, as I watched the guards build up in numbers outside our block as they prepared to search it.

'Christ, we're in it now,' said the Chook. 'Maybe if we say we're all poofs. Yeah, we could say we're all fags and we snuck into this cell to gang bang the Jap while he was asleep. What do you think?'

The Don had baited Musaki the night before with a heavy dose of sleepers and the bloke was sprawled out on his mattress on the floor, deep in dreamland. There was no way that we were going to trust this guy.

The plot had been to load up Musaki with downers and when he woke up the next morning, long after we were gone, he could plead ignorance and scream out for his embassy. After all, the bloke was caught with a kilogram of heroin and only sentenced to six years imprisonment. The Chook was caught with 32 grams of hashish and was sentenced to 17 years, so as far as the Japs were concerned they were basically untouchable.

The guards started to fumble with the locks on the front doors of our block, trying to find the key that fitted.

'Porca Madonna,' sighed the Don.

'Don't freak out, you fucking wog,' the Chook whispered with a hiss in his voice, then looked at me. 'What do ya reckon, Russ, we tell 'em we just snuck in here to gang bang the Jap, do you think they'll believe us?'

'We're all dressed in dark clothes, our faces are blackened with candle soot and the bar on the Nip's window is cut away – I find your story hard to believe, 86,' I said.

'But what if I jump out and start kissing the fuckers, like you did in the office that day, yeah, we could all just run out and start kissing the fuckers, what do you say?' the Chook replied, as he looked at the Don. 'What do you say hey, Guiseppe?'

'Porca Madonna, Jesus Kristus,' the Don replied.

Things started to change outside as the prison director became really pissed off and started to yell at the guard with the keys, then turned around and stormed off closely, followed by a full platoon of guards.

'Porca Madonna, they gotta the wrong keys, they no gotta the right keys to search the block, if I live 100 more years I never believe this shit, they no gotta the right keys,' Guiseppe whispered.

'Fucking fantastic,' I said. 'Come on Chook, let's get back to our cells and we'll try again tomorrow night if all goes well.' Off we dashed back to our cells, replacing the bars and quickly gluing them back.

The following morning I covered up the glue marks on both mine and the Chook's cell bars. When I went over to the Don's cell, he was a nervous wreck. I glued back the bars on his cell and carefully covered up the glue marks.

'No wonder you wogs lost the war,' the Chook said. 'We have a little problem like last night and you go all flakey.'

'Who's a flakey? Who's a flakey? You wanna fight? OK, I giva you a fight,' the Don growled as he stood up off the floor ready to blue with the Chook.

'Settle down, both of you. Chook, fuck off. Go check the rabbits. Don, better you stay in the cell. Here take one of those downers and sleep the day away, I'll tell everyone you're sick OK, but stay in the cell. That window bar isn't glued in strong, and we don't want Musaki pulling on it when he wakes up. On second thoughts, you had better not take a downer unless you're sure our little Nippon mate is going to sleep the day away too, you need to keep your eyes on him. I've got to go to the kitchen and help Kim get the food together, OK,' I said.

'Yeah, yeah, thanks, I stay here, Russ, no worries. I am no flakey, Russ. Porca Madonna, last night, I no believa they gotta the wrong keys,' he said and started to smile.

'Yeah, pretty far out hey, but we try again tonight,' I said as I smiled back and headed off to the kitchen.

The following night we tried again. When all the block was asleep the Chook patted on the wall of my cell.

'Ready?' he said.

'Ready,' I replied.

The Don's blackened face appeared from the folds of the sarongs that were nailed up over the bars of his and Musaki's cell.

The Chook and I looked at each other. I gave him a wink and said 'now'.

We pulled the bars loose and just as we were squeezing through them, there was a God almighty scream from one of the cells to my right.

We both froze where we were, half in and half out of our cells, then there was another scream that shattered the stillness of the night.

I looked over at the Don and he started to replace the bar that was to give us the entry we needed into his cell. I gave the Chook a quick look and we read each other's minds – another fuck-up.

I quickly retreated back to my cell and as I was replacing the bar, the whole block started to wake. Within half an hour, there were about 20 local prisoners banging on the bars of their cells.

When the guards turned up to see what the problem was, they found one of the prisoners suffering extreme stomach pain. This particular prisoner was one of the more wealthy slimebags who had the money to bribe the guards to take him to the hospital. It turned out he was immediately admitted and underwent an operation to remove his appendix.

Once again, our escape bid was put off.

The following day I rushed around repairing the bloody bars again and when I arrived in the Don's cell, Musaki was half awake – well he was sitting up on his mattress anyway.

He had spent the past two days doped out of his head, so I suppose he had to wake up sooner or later for a shit and a piss, not to mention some food.

It was after Musaki had returned from the toilet and sat down to eat some porridge that he said, 'I had a dream the other night that you were all in my cell, ha, strange, ha, strange, this porridge needs sugar, tastes strange, ha, my tongue, see my tongue,' he said as he poked out what looked like a liver with a white fur coat. 'Ha, tastes strange,' he said as he polished off his bowl of porridge, skolled his coffee and went back to sleep.

'Russell,' the Don said when Musaki started to snore, 'if we don't go tonight, I no gotta any more downers. I give the last to Musaki, just now in the porridge.'

'Yeah, how many did you give him?' I asked.

'Five 6 mgs,' Don replied.

'Shit, I slipped four of them into his coffee when I gave him the sugar, so that's a total of nine, 6 mgs of Lexotans. Shit, that should keep him on the deck until this time tomorrow,' I said.

'Oh fuck, now you blokes tell me,' the Chook said. 'Why didn't you tell me before? I just gave the cunt a whole strip.'

'How the Christ did you manage that?' I asked.

'I thought you had used up all you had on the Nasi Padangs, Russ, and when the Don said that he was nearly out of them, because Musaki was eating them like smarties, I thought I'd slip that strip of Lexies you gave me into the hot water for his coffee. Christ, do you think we've OD'd the poor bastard?' Chook said.

'Christ, that's 19, 6 mg Lexatons in one hit, not to mention all the rest that he's had over the past two days. It's a lot, Chook,' I said.

'Oh, Porca Madonna,' the Don sighed.

'Any ideas?' the Chook said to me.

'A suicide note would be nice,' I replied, 'but it would have to be written in Japanese, it's the only way; if we wrote it in English they would suss us out.'

'Yeah, that's not a bad idea, we could leave it in the cell when we fucked off. Look, I'll just nip over to Atsushi's cell,' the Chook said and started to smile. 'Nip over, get it, nip over? Yeah, well anyway, I'll just nip over and see if I can con Atsushi into helping me write a suicide letter to my Japanese girlfriend.'

Atsushi was another one of the Japanese prisoners, he was all but four foot tall, with a shadow that was probably heavier than him – well it sure looked a lot fatter.

'You didn't tell me you had a Japanese girlfriend, Chook,' I said.

'No, well I don't, not yet anyway, but if I ever do get one it could be handy to have a quick suicide note in my pocket. What do you think, Don?'

'You crazy, the man, she's a going to die, we gotta tell the guards, we gotta get a doctor, the man, she'll die if we don a do something,' said the Don.

'It's not a she Don, it's a he,' the Chook growled, 'and if you call the guards, you'll die, because I'll fucking kill you personally. I've got 17 years, mate and Russ has 20, it's him–' pointing at Musaki's sleeping body '–or us, so shut the fuck up, OK!'

'I'll arrange a suicide note through Atsushi,' the Chook said as he looked over towards me.

'Don't go flakey man,' he said to the Don as he got up and left the cell.

'I a no murderer, I can't a kill this man, I no can a just sit here and let him a die,' the Don said when the Chook was gone.

'Then don't,' I said, 'help me flush that shit out of his belly.'

Within half an hour we had Musaki spewing his guts up all over the cell floor.

A couple of hours later, when the cell was cleaned up and Musaki was again sleeping peacefully, Chook returned with the suicide note written in Japanese.

'This place smells like spew,' he said, then looked at the Don. 'You nearly panicked Don, and you nearly fucked up our chances of getting out of this piss pit – you're an old junkie and you should know better. All Musaki needed was a good spew, not the guards. Russ and I were just playing with you, you fuckwit. Here stick this letter in Musaki's pocket or under his pillow; it's a suicide note all right, covering his arse after we fuck off tonight through his cell.' Once again the Chook left in a huff.

As I've said before, there was a lot that the Chook and I could say to each other with only the quickest of glances.

He was the closest to me in those days, not only a friend, but more of what you would call a kindred spirit. A bloke who knows your moods, so he knows when to sidestep you if you're cranky, or drop in when you're feeling blue, and vice versa.

The friendship that I had with the Chook was well . . . I suppose you could compare it with the friendship of politicians of the same party. We were both allowed to badmouth each other, but if someone tried to pull our whole government down along with our system, we stuck together. That's what our relationship was like – we both had a set task and that task was getting our arses out of Indonesia, no matter how. I guess that's why we worked so closely together during those years; like all those politicians, we united to fight the common foe: prison.

On the night of 28 December 1987, the Chook, the Don and I broke out of Krobokan Prison on the Island of Bali in Indonesia. Why that date and all these particulars are still so vivid in my mind, I do not know.

I had surely suffered worse and been in many more dire situations before this imprisonment. My ears still ring to the thud of the 105-millimetre Howitzer shells that fell on the city of Da Nang in the 1970s. I can still taste that burnt-acid flavour of cordite and gunpowder in the back of my throat as magazines and empty clips were changed for new full ones. They were the days of a young man who held no fear of death. I was invincible. What was death to me in those days? Nothing more than a short sleep and I was too busy to sleep.

It is only now that I am an older man nearing his fifth decade of life, that I recall so many of my memories, search them and reflect back on them. Now I know that nobody is invincible.

CHAPTER 7

SHADOW PEOPLE

No man knows his own courage
Until it's tested

It was just past 03.00 hours when the Chook and I gathered together in the Don's cell, all in black and all with blackened faces. There were three cars arranged, one for the Chook, one for the Don and one for me.

The Don crawled out of the window first, followed closely by the Chook. After they had left the cell I checked out Musaki as he was ripping out the Z's on his mattress on the floor. There was nothing wrong with this bloke and the downers were having no adverse effects.

It was just as I was climbing out of the cell window that I heard the crack – it sounded like a rifle shot.

Once I managed to clear myself of the window, I dashed behind a small bush and huddled down, as still and as silent as possible. For a brief moment the rain ceased; all I could hear was my own heartbeat. It seemed that the torrential downpour had just been turned off, as if by God's own hand.

'No, no,' I thought, 'Please don't stop now, rain, oh please heavens open up. I need you . . . yes, that's it, that's it.' As if the clouds had heard me the rain started again and soon became a flood-like downpour. (This rain would have impressed Noah!)

I looked around and could see the Don hanging from the barbed wire that surrounded the tops of the prison walls. He was trying to pull himself up over the wall, as a searchlight passed over him and hit the wall and roof of our block. The guard in Tower 3 was making sweeps of the prison compound with his searchlight.

I caught sight of Chook dashing down along one of the storm drains and thought to myself, don't run, you fucker, don't run, stay still and let the light cross over you. The search beam was lowered and started to sweep partly across the wall and then partly across the storm drain.

I was still squatting down in one of the vegetable patches as I watched the beam of light pass over the drain, where the Chook had run. The light followed the drain and then pulled back to the vegetable patch.

I stayed motionless as the light passed over me, then looked up at the wall where the Don was hanging.

The searchlight went back down and followed the drain again, but my eyes were locked on the Don hanging from the barbed wire on the top of the prison walls. As I watched, his body seemed to come alive and he started to pull himself up, up higher onto the wall. I knew that the barbs on the wire must have been tearing the shit out of his hands, but he managed to get one leg over the wall and, once he had a solid hold, he pulled himself over and squeezed between the barbed-wire strands (and the broken glass that was embedded along the top of the wall) and pushed himself through to the other side. All I could see then were his arms and hands. He released the barbed wire and slid down the other side, to the side of freedom.

I waited a good five minutes for the sounds of the sirens, bells and alarms to start ringing. Nothing happened. As soon as the searchlight was switched off I made my way over to where the ladder was lying on the ground.

Christ, wasn't I pissed off! The loud crack that I had heard, and I am sure half the world must have heard also, was the sound of the ladder breaking. That explained why the Don was hanging from the barbed wire on the wall – just as he reached the wire, the ladder must have given way and left him dangling. No wonder the Chook took off faster than any of the rabbits could have run, bolting crouched down at full speed along the storm drain heading for the office.

We had discussed an emergency plan over the previous month. If anything went wrong once we were out of our cells and in the prison compound, we'd decided the best place to bolt to was where the guards would come from.

All of the guards were in the prison office, apart from those still in the watchtowers that were mounted along the prison walls. I knew that the Chook would attempt to climb up onto the roof of the prison offices and, from there, try to drop down into the outside carpark. It was a dodgy move, but if the shit were to hit the fan, there would've been at least a chance of pulling it off by going that way. It was better than just holding up your hands and giving up to the bastards.

It was all pretty dangerous though. To get up on the roof of the prison offices, you had to pass the odd wandering patrol within the prison compound, then climb up the drainpipe that ran up the wall to the roof and behind that wall were a good dozen or more guards. Then you had to cross the tin roof above their heads without making a sound so as to access the wall. Then there was the fact that the carpark was right in the front of the prison offices where the guards played cards and sucked piss all night.

The nitty gritty of it all was that the route that the Chook had just taken left a lot to be desired. The chances of pulling it off were slim.

The problem that faced me now was how the hell was I going to get over the wall?

I gave the broken ladder a quick check over and noticed that one of the long three-by-three poles had broken away cleanly from the rest of the ladder, or should I say the rabbits' roof.

Sticking out from the top of one end were two big six-inch nails, bent in the form of a hook. I picked up the wooden pole and set off towards one of the darker sides of the prison walls where one of the lights that ran along it was broken.

I dropped into the storm drain and criss-crossed the prison compound in a number of places, then dashed along through the shit and garbage that had been collected in the storm drain during the monsoon season of that year and headed for number three watchtower. This was the quiet side of the prison, where the grass was long and the mud was thick, and I knew I was less likely to bump into one of the prison's roving patrols. The Indonesian guards liked to stay dry and keep their shoes clean, so I knew from over a year of watching the rice suckers that they all did their best to avoid duty in Tower 3.

It took me nearly an hour to get there because twice I had to crawl past guards who were sheltering under the eaves of the prison blocks from the rain.

I was grateful for the rain, even though it was filling up the storm drains. The square cement storm drains, even when clean, only measured about half a metre wide by three quarters of a metre high. They would normally be cleaned out once or twice a year, if lucky. However, as usual, being the Murphy's Law graduate that I am, the drains looked and smelt like they hadn't been touched since the Second World War! As most of the drainage pipes throughout the prison were open, the changing seasons would ensure a thick growth of just about anything that would attach itself to the cement walls; fungus, mould, vomit, shit, decayed animals and whatever else you can think of flourished in these drains. At one point I became stuck and thought I was going to drown but managed to get free and clear of the water.

When I reached number three watchtower, I slowly stood up from the storm drain, the rain belting down around me, my face blackened, with bits and pieces of leaves and twigs sticking to me, along with this long shroud of stringy-type moss, that hung from my shoulders like a long cape. The storm drain had camouflaged me well. As a bolt of lightning cracked through the jet-black sky, I looked down upon my body and what I saw of myself through the electrified heavens boosted me to new heights.

I had truly become one with the night. It was my friend, it was my ally, and I was now a living, breathing, unstoppable shadow of this night. Nothing could stop me short of death.

I slipped the two-metre pole up onto the bars of the watchtower and pulled myself up it. When my hands found the steel bars that ran around the sides of the tower, I pulled myself up onto the walkway. If you've got a gun, you bastard, you better use it now, I thought, as I slid into the watchtower.

I slowly moved my body over into another shadow and stood up, searching for the guard. I didn't have to search too long or too far – after all a prison watchtower isn't all that big.

The guard was having a piss over the wall on the opposite side of where I had climbed up. I watched him as he did up his zip and wandered back into the enclosed part of the watchtower. He picked up a packet of cigarettes, pulled one out and crossed over to where I was standing. As he passed me, he lit up his dotch and walked by onto the catwalk where I had just pulled myself up. I could see the stick that I had used still hanging from the catwalk bars by the bent nails. 'Kill him, kill him now,' said a little voice in the back of my mind, 'kill him and run.'

'No, no not yet, there is no need to,' said another little voice. 'Take it to the max, see how far you can go, after all you are just a shadow. He doesn't even know you're here. Feel him, feel him out.'

I stood there in the shadow of a shadow and watched as the guard turned around and once again passed me by. He sat down on a chair, pulled out a small transistor radio and tuned into a channel playing Indonesian *dunduk* music.

I watched him as his head was nodding to the music. He reached and pulled out a small half-empty bottle of Mansion House whisky from the pocket of his jacket that was hanging on a nail stuck next to one of the windows.

I could've pissed off then and there but for some odd unknown reason I just had to stay and test myself.

I silently crept up behind the guard and slipped my arm around his throat, blocking his neck and cutting off his air supply, holding him down on the floor as his legs were kicking like a thrashing machine and his hands were trying to claw at my face. The wind outside the guard post was roaring and the rain was thundering down like a crescendo of jungle drums.

'Kill him, kill him,' cried a wild voice in the back of my mind, 'kill the fucker, kill him now that you've got the chance.'

'No, no you've proved your point. You don't need to kill him, let him go, let him go,' said the better half of me.

I released the guard and headed off over the wall with visions of freedom in my mind.

'Run, run, run, run,' I said to myself.

That morning I ran 28 kilometres for freedom but it wasn't far enough. Destiny and Murphy's Law had other plans.

After the Chook managed to climb up over the guards and avoid who knows how many foot patrols in the prison compound, he was caught no more than 200 metres from the prison. They sprung him at 05.30 in the morning, and once he was caught the alarm was sent out, though I didn't know that at the time. I had only reached the Oberoi Hotel near Kuta by the time every policeman and every soldier on Bali had begun looking for both Guiseppe and myself.

Don't forget that Indonesia is a police state, or should I say a military state. The whole country suffers military madness – it's what they call a guided democracy. Guided by one bloke, President Soeharto, and his wife and kids. They owned the place in those days, but politics were the least of my concerns, all that was in my mind was to get the hell out of the country as quickly as I could.

I had two very good passports on me, one for a British male and the other for a New Zealand female, along with two international driver's licences.

I had planned to leave the country as a woman and for me it would've been easy – for the two years in Krobokan Prison I had not cut my hair. It was very long, but only a few people knew just how long it was because I kept it tied up in a top knot, like the Indian Sikhs do. I was very boyish looking, which with a little make-up could easily become a little girlish.

A few days before, with the help of the Chook, I had dyed and permed my hair and then hidden the fact with the beanie I always wore. My face in those days was all but hairless and though I used to sport a thin moustache and a small goatee beard, both could easily be removed. I had also shaved my legs (they were probably the hairiest part of my body in those days).

The photo in the New Zealand passport was of one of my blue-eyed blonde sisters. I knew that I could make myself look like one of my sisters, even if it wasn't 100 per cent identical. I knew that to Asians most Europeans or Westerners look alike, just as most Asians look alike to Europeans or Westerners.

When I reached the area of the Oberoi Hotel, I went down to the beach. Still dressed in black with a blackened face, I dived into the water to clean myself up and to discard the dark clothes I was wearing in the ocean, weighing them down with rocks.

I swam down towards the Oberoi Hotel and when I emerged from the sea I was wearing a long blouse-like shirt with a belt around the waist, and my long hair hanging down.

Looking now more like a woman, I headed for the ladies' toilets that were right next to the swimming pool, no more than 200 metres from the surf. I was carrying a small cloth shoulder bag that held all that I would need to make my transformation from a guy into a girl complete.

As I headed to the women's toilet I pulled out a book that I had, along with other things, sealed up in waterproof plastic zip bags. The book I had was the Bible.

I had learned from previous experiences that the best place to hide your face when someone is looking for you, or at you, is in a book, newspaper or magazine, but a book suited me better. It was easier to carry and it was a special book, not only because it was a Bible but within the cover of it I had stashed $1,300, a British passport and the spare international driver's licence. I buried my face in the Bible as I headed to the women's toilet, hiding the lower part of my face from one of the early morning hotel staff who was preparing the tables by the poolside for the early morning guests.

As I passed him, the dirty little bastard made a rude comment in Indonesian and smiled. Christ, I thought, I haven't even got the bra on yet and this little bastard is trying to pick me up.

Man, that waiter would have shit himself if I had lowered the book, showing my moustache and goatee, given him a wink and said, 'Dan saya cinta kamajuga ['And I love you also'].' That would have really blown him away.

When I arrived in the ladies toilets the first thing that I had to do was have a shave; however the rotten bloody razor wasn't in with all the other goodies of importance that I had so carefully packed into the shoulder bag.

Oh fuck, I thought, of all the stupid things to happen. I had given the Chook a loan of the razor the night before and had forgotten to get the damn thing back. (Here was another great fuck-up to add to the Best Plans of Mice and Men.)

I decided that maybe I could pluck all the hairs out of my moustache and goatee with a pair of tweezers, but this proved fruitless – and painful. After plucking out one side of my moustache my top lip was all swollen and bleeding, not to mention the eye above it being full of tears.

Fuck it, I thought, there's another razor waiting in the car that Gary had stashed for me. I'll just have to have a shave when I get there otherwise I'll end up here until next week, and probably look like the world's roughest woman.

So off I went, exiting the women's toilets with the Bible held firmly in my hands. As I passed the pool I noticed that the cheeky little waiter was bending over the pool trying to retrieve a table napkin that the wind had blown into it. I had a quick look around to see if there was anyone in sight, but the place was still empty so, as I passed him, I gave him a quick

HELL'S PRISONER

push. The splash I heard behind me as I walked away made me feel a little better.

I walked along the beach about a kilometre or two, heading to Kuta and the car, when out of the blue appeared a prison guard moonlighting as a statue seller. The little prick came from nowhere. There were less than five or six people on the beach that early in the morning.

The bastard must have been hiding under the sand, I thought, as he thrust a statue in my face saying, 'Does this pretty lady want to buy this very cheap ivory carving? It's very cheap because it's my first sale of the day. Just make me an off . . . oh, sorry sir,' he said as the shit-arsed statue that he thrust into my face knocked away the bloody Bible that I was holding up, and I realised who he was.

I still had the Bible in my hand after I had left the Oberoi Hotel, holding it up to my face, hoping that people would just think I was engrossed in the book, or maybe very religious.

'Ah, no thank you,' I said and kept on walking, but I had noticed his face change as he looked at me.

He recognised me, as someone he thought he knew, but he couldn't quite place from where.

I kept on walking for about 10 more metres when he ran up to me, swung me around and yelled, 'Russell, Russell.'

As I faced him with my most innocent of smiles, I said, 'Who? You've made a . . .' Before I even got the sentence out, he reached behind his back and I knew he was going for a weapon.

With that I finished the sentence, 'mistake', and swung a back-handed closed fist across his jaw.

As he fell to the ground I took off, managing to make a good 50 or 60 metres before I heard the first shots ring out.

The little bastard had his gun on him, that's illegal, I thought, as I started to zigzag across the beach. As I heard something *bizzzzz* through the air above my head, I changed course and headed for the coconut trees and foliage that ran alongside the white sands of Kuta Beach. I noticed a small foot trail that ran through the scrub onto the beach, and as I ran up it I ran smack bang into two policemen on a motorcycle. The one in the pillion seat was carrying a rifle.

They were cutting quick and I was travelling as fast as my legs could carry me.

When we met, I had the advantage. I could jump, they could only stop, which would have taken them time on that narrow path. There was no way that they could have turned, or they would have ploughed into the coconut trees.

I jumped, but not away from them, kicking straight out at the rider. As he flew back he knocked the pillion off, the rifle sailed into the air and the bike headed straight into the coconut trees, smashing itself.

Within seconds I was on my feet and, after seeing another motorcycle coming up the track loaded with more coppers, I ran back to the beach. I was thinking of trying to stash myself in the scrub, but there were too many small huts scattered along the area and too many locals there who would give me up.

By the time I got back to the beach I could see an MP truck half full of military policemen, cutting off one section of the beach and as I looked over towards the other end of the beach, a beat-up old MP truck appeared spewing out more military police. By fuck they're fast, I thought. How did they get it together so quickly? It seemed I had really underestimated the bludgers.

When I looked up from where I was hiding I could see the runway of Bali's international airport sticking out like a finger into the sea and on its runway I could clearly see a plane getting ready for take-off.

I can catch that plane, I thought, it doesn't matter where it's going, but I can catch it. All I have to do is swim but it would have to be a long swim. How many kilometres? Five, ten, maybe more.

I heard the beating in the bush behind me and the yelling of dozens of voices coming from the MPs who were searching for me, with the help of the local village people of course.

My only choice was take the long swim or give myself up.

I opted for the long swim. As I dashed for the surf I heard a voice yell out, 'Sana, Sana, Di Sana,' and the sand all around me erupted, followed by sounds that most people would only hear on cracker night.

'Run, run, run,' screamed an all-empowering voice in my mind, 'run, run, run.'

Is this how my old friend Andy felt, as he raced into those bullets that day in Da Nang? My mind flashed back to the evacuation of that Vietnamese coastal city.

When my feet reached the water, I was forced to slow down on my wild run into the ocean, as the waves started to bash against me, trying to throw me back onto the beach.

The water started splashing all around me as if people were throwing stones at me, but I knew that it wasn't stones being thrown.

As I dived into the first big wave, which covered me completely, I started to swim underwater towards the airport. I swam as far as I could underwater, my lungs on the verge of bursting, and I resurfaced with only my head sticking out of the water.

The surf was up, but not the surf for a surfboard rider. The previous night's rain and the general bad weather had gotten the sea into a turmoil. The undercurrent was enormous and I battled with it for nearly an hour. I could feel it dragging me away from the airport and out to sea.

You can do it, I told myself, you can, you must, you have to.

Just get to that bloody plane, I had locked in my mind.

If I could grab hold of one of the wheels, I could tie myself onto one of the wheel struts, people had escaped from the Eastern bloc countries doing the same thing. Sure some of them died, but some of them made it too, the ones who didn't freeze to death or fall out of the undercarriage.

So don't forget to tie yourself in, at least you won't fall out of the plane when it makes it's landing, and if you freeze to death, well, that's the risk you take, but don't drown. No, no, I must not drown, I thought.

Swim, swim, I told myself, but as hard as I tried, the further and further the airport and land became. Then the cramps started – first in the calves of my leg muscles, then up into my thighs. I tried to massage them away, but my mouth and nose only started to fill up with salt water.

Float, float, try to float, I told myself, relax and try to float on your back. But the waves wouldn't allow it. As my legs cramped up for what I thought would be the last time, and the undertow started to take me down, I could hear bells ringing in my ears – they weren't unpleasant bells, they were more like music.

Yeah, I suppose I could only describe them as musical bells. I've heard that drowning isn't all that unpleasant a death, and I really wasn't afraid of death, after all, it's something we all must experience at one time of our lives. Just as the music of the bells was reaching its crescendo, I saw the hull of a dug-out fishing boat with outriggers drop down into the waves. I held up my arm to it, waving it farewell as I started to sink below the waves.

When I opened my eyes, I was lying on my back in a thin-hulled native fishing boat, looking at a little white woolly haired old man pushing down on my stomach while I spewed salt water all over the place. As my mind cleared I could see that there were three policemen in the boat – I had been recaptured, but I was too weak to do anything about it, except vomit up more salt water.

When I was returned to Krobokan Prison, my reception left a lot to be desired. I definitely wasn't treated like the returning lost child. The beating that I got from the guards on that day I'll not go into too deeply, as it only opens up old wounds that I am doing my best to forget about, but I was beaten well that day.

My clothes, which were admittedly only a pair of underpants, a long shirt and a belt, were stripped off. I was dragged over a table with my hands in handcuffs and my legs pulled down around the table legs where I was sprawled spread-eagled.

That's when the guards laid into me.

'So you want to run away, you want to use these legs to run away,' they yelled and screamed, as they smashed into my kneecaps and beat the skin off my shins.

I was to be an example to any other prisoners who may try to escape in future so I was dragged up and down block C by the handcuffs, the iron edges of which cut deeply painfully into my wrists as I was dragged by the hair. Each guard had his turn at dragging me across the floor, while the other guards kicked the shit out of me or stomped down on my back, trying to break my backbone. As the day drew on I realised that half the guards were not in uniform, and that they were from all of the shifts.

You maggots, I thought, you're all so brave now, but when alone you're all so fucking gutless, you race of fucking maggots.

All of the guards knew of our escape bid, and had heard that we all had been recaptured.

The Don had been picked up sitting on the beach and had given up without a fight. In fact, he had even handed over the passport that I had doctored up for him along with the bloody map that he had, detailing how to get to the car that was waiting for him. But that didn't stop the guards from beating the shit out of him too.

When I found out, I was fuming at the thought that the Don would give up so easily, after all we had gone through, and then to hand over the fucking passport and map, without any form of resistance. The only good point of that day was the sound of the Don's screams as the guards beat the shit out of him and finally crushed his cheekbone, knocking the bastard out.

At least being knocked out, he couldn't be hurt any more, and better still couldn't talk.

It was after the Don stopped screaming and the bulk of the guards came out of his cell that they returned to me. They pulled me off the floor and spread me on top of the table again. This time I was on my belly, and they went to work on the backs of my legs and buttocks with their nightsticks and batons. I screamed and I screamed and I screamed, not only to satisfy the guards, because I knew that if I didn't scream it would only piss them off more, and they had their egos at stake. But I also screamed in pain, frustration and, above all, I screamed in hate.

After what seemed like a lifetime of screams and pain, I was finally pulled off the table again and dragged into a bare cell.

Four guards held me up in the cell and my old mate Darma went to work on my face, with his fist. Believe it or not (because I couldn't) I was still conscious. I watched him back off for a moment, shaking one of his blood-covered hands. I could only see him through one eye because the other was swollen closed. When he pulled a nightstick from one of the guards he was trembling in a blood-lust rage and he started to bash me over the head.

Bright burning stars appeared in the blackness of my mind and my ears were ringing. I am not sure how many blows I could feel, or suffered, but the next thing I knew I was lying on the floor, curled up in the foetal position with the guards all kicking me.

One kick caught me right in the balls and the pain shook my whole body. My bloody balls were sticking out behind me and the guard, or guards just kept kicking them until, by a stroke of luck, they kicked them back between my legs. That last kick I received into the old family jewels made me start to spew my guts up.

There was blood everywhere, I couldn't tell what I was spewing up, my liver, my kidneys, my tongue or my balls. Then one kick caught me in the side of the head and I could feel myself blown into a great dark void.

The pain stopped and so too did the screams and yells of the prison guards. I remember my last thought was, so this is death, what a cunt of a way to meet it, kicked to death like a dog.

CHAPTER 8

GOODBYE, CUSTARD APPLES

Pity for others is a rare commodity
Self pity . . . ah, that comes in abundance

Hazy thoughts came with clink, clink, clunk, clunk, screech. The door needs oil, I thought, then a flashlight was passed over my body.

'*Munkin mati,*' a voice said behind the flashlight's beam.

'Maybe dead, yeah, maybe he's dead. Let's check out the other two white dogs,' said another voice and the guards left my cell, clink, clink, screech, clink, clang.

The door needs some oil . . . yes, the door needs some oil, and I am not dead, you fuckers. I am not dead yet, I thought, and passed out.

The following morning when I woke up I didn't know where I was, or even who I was for that matter. I could only hear the tweeting of a bird far up somewhere on the prison block.

As I opened my one good eye and looked along the floor, my mind started to play tricks on me. All I could see was an ocean of blood, an ocean of thick congealed blood, and what appeared to be lots of little blue helicopters taking off and landing on it.

I watched for what seemed ages, as these little blue helicopters landed on one spot on this crimson ocean, then took off and landed somewhere else. I then noticed that the ocean stopped after a while and plain sheets of grey led to a wall. A dirty wall all splashed with black, maroon and red, and the helicopters were landing on them too.

'Where am I?' I thought, 'Who am I, and how can helicopters land on a wall?'

'Russell, Russell, Russ, can you hear me?' a voice said. 'Russ, Russ, hey Russ, are you OK?'

'Who's that? Do I know that voice? What's happened? Where am I? Who's Russ? Why can't I move my arms?' All these questions ran through my mind as I tried to get up, but the pain rushed through my body in a torrent, enabling me only to groan.

Oh, Christ, I thought as I tried to move, and I let my face fall back into the ocean of blood to watch the helicopters take off and land. It was only when one of them went up my nose, and I snorted it out, that I realised that it wasn't a helicopter at all, it was a rotten little blowfly. That's when the events of the previous day all started to rush back through my mind.

'Russ, Russ, mate, it's me, the Chook. Are you OK? Are you OK, mate? Say something, fucking say something. If you can't talk, at least moan again. That was you who moaned before, wasn't it? Hey Russ, make a sound, any sound, cough, shit, spew, fart, anything, just make a sound,' he pleaded. 'Just make a fucking sound, mate, anything!'

'They're not helicopters,' I groaned. 'They're big, but they're not helicopters.'

'Say again, I didn't catch it. Where's the helicopters?' the Chook replied, in a voice that I could feel had lost some of its alarm at me not answering earlier.

'I can't move, I think my legs are broken,' I said.

'If that's all that's broken you're fucking lucky! I thought the fuckers had killed you. Take it easy, mate, we'll get out of here, there'll always be another time. A time when we can pay these fuckers back,' he said.

Yeah I thought, there will always be another time, Darma, and when it comes I'll be there.

My mind was going off at a thousand thoughts a minute, all of which could do me no good. All I could think of was how I'd kill those guards, and those 22 bullshitting witnesses who had all so blatantly lied about me, not to mention how I'd pay back those low-life policemen who had set me up in the first place.

But lying naked on a cold floor with my hands chained up behind my back in an empty cell, with litres of congealing blood all around me and my body screaming in pain at the slightest move, I was a far cry from a man who could fulfil a payback.

I couldn't even swat that rotten little fly that kept trying to climb up my nose, but I was still alive and life breeds hope. So I set about getting my first revenge – on the fly that was trying to set up house in my nostril.

I laid back and did my best to relax and, as the fly built up its courage, I let it climb further and further into my nose. When it had got nearly an inch up, I slowly brought up my shoulder and turned my head. Believe me, this simple manoeuvre hurt like shit, but when I crushed the little bastard by pushing my shoulder against my nose, it was as good a feeling as winning the bloody Melbourne Cup.

When I blew that fly's dead body out of my nostril, my head started spinning and pain shot through my face – but it felt good. This was my first victory for a long, long time. I know that this must sound stupid or crazy, but it's not. You see, the mind needs its little victories if it is to keep functioning, otherwise it will just collapse totally. In the position I was in at the time my mind definitely needed a boost because that's all I had left. That little victory over a fly gave me the strength I needed.

My body was chained and broken, and as the days passed I checked out the damage that I had physically suffered. I basically took inventory.

One eye was badly swollen and I couldn't see out of it at all, but I forced the thought of it being permanently damaged out of my mind. Thoughts like that could not help me.

My hands were still handcuffed behind my back and my fingers felt like sausages, but at least I could move them. I started to stretch my legs but the pain was excruciating. It took me nearly two hours to stretch them out completely, and while I was in the process the guards came in.

I could hear them coming as they unlocked the first doors that led into the block, so I quickly folded up my legs again (which hurt like all Christ). I lay back on the cell floor dropping my face into the pool of old congealed blood. One guard gave me a quick look over, while others unlocked the Don's cell and took him away.

When the block had been locked up again the Chook whispered, 'Russ, Russ, they've taken the Don away.'

'Yeah, I know,' I said, 'I caught sight of him out of the side of my eye and he was walking.'

'But did you see his face?' the Chook asked.

'No, only his legs, but they were working pretty good though,' I replied.

'He looked like fucking Quasimodo,' the Chook said and then went silent.

The Don was the last of my problems at the time. I had to find out what was broken in my own body. Once again I started to try to stretch out my legs. When I got them stretched out in front of me my mind started to reel, not through pain but at what I saw.

Between my legs was a little wrinkled penis, doing its best to hide itself from the huge shining mass of skin that was underneath it. My testicles and the old scrotum bag were swollen to the size of nearly two tennis balls.

As I stared at them I couldn't believe their size, but the really weird thing was that they didn't hurt as much as other parts of my body. Sure they hurt, but nowhere near as bad as my back, where my kidneys once lived.

I stared at them in wonderment for a while, then followed my legs down with my one good eye to my toes, half of which were blue, yellow and green, with a few black spots on them. My shins were all covered in blood and my kneecaps were so swollen that the skin stretched around them was shining.

When the guards returned with the Don, all I could do was fall back on my handcuffed arms, into the blood that was as thick as jelly on my cell floor, and close my eyes.

The guards threw the Don back into his cell and then came to check me out. I could hear their gasps of astonishment as they looked into my cell and saw my balls.

The Chook was the next to be taken out.

'By Christ,' I heard the Chook say as he stared into my cell, 'What the fuck have you done to him?'

'The same that we'll do to you,' one of the guards laughed as they dragged the Chook away to the prison office to be questioned and cross-examined about our escape.

When they had gone I lifted my head up, looked at my balls, and passed out.

I remained in that state until the next day. I woke up to find the guards already in my cell. One of them was taking the handcuffs off me. A flash of pain ran through my hands and then into every finger, as the blood started to flow back into them. A vial of something vile was stuck under my nose and I was dragged over towards one of the cell walls.

Bawana, the prison doctor, was there. He had a look of worry on his face as he held my hands and started to massage them, giving fleeting looks at my newly acquired tennis balls.

He shaved part of my head and applied butterfly stitches to the gaping wounds. Once he had cleaned them of the shit, dirt and encrusted blood, he gave me two injections. He then cleaned up my one good eye, and shone a light into it.

'Enough! This man needs to go to a hospital. I'll not be held responsible,' Bawana announced.

'You won't be. You know how to fill out your reports,' replied one of the guards, as he pushed me back on the floor, pulling my hands behind my back, and getting out the handcuffs again.

'If you put those handcuffs on as tight as they were before, he will lose his hands. That would be very hard to explain if his embassy were to question it,' Bawana said.

'Then why don't you put them on!' the guard replied.

So Bawana replaced my handcuffs. I could feel him run his fingers all around the insides of them once they were locked on – he had locked them on very loosely.

As they were all leaving the cell, I looked up from where I was on the blood-covered floor and said, 'Thanks, Doc.'

Bawana paused then looked back at me and said in English, which none of the present guards could understand fully, 'You're in pain, aren't you?' It was not really a question, it was more of a statement. I could only nod my head.

He then returned to where I was lying on the floor, opened up his bag as he kneeled beside me and pulled out a syringe and ampoule.

'This is a morphine injection. It will help relieve the pain, though I am sure you know what it is, being a narcotic case!' Bawana said. 'I'll try to come back tomorrow,' he continued as he placed the syringe and broken ampoule into his bag, then headed off out of the cell.

As he left, I fell into the sleep and the dreams of a painless slumber induced by old mother morphine.

I dreamt of a Wall of Blood and of Sheryl, the mother of my children, splashing the blood on the walls with her paintbrush as fast as I tried to clean it off.

'Please don't do this, Sheryl, please, please, please, there has been too much blood, please, stop, please stop,' I cried.

But the blue helicopters appeared and refilled her easel and the buckets that were at her feet with fresh blood. As I frantically tried to wash the white wall clean, she would splash more blood on it.

When I woke up the next day on the cell floor, the dream still vivid in my

ABOVE: This is a photo of Eddy (not Eddy the nun-killer) and myself taken in Malang Prison, Central Highlands of Java, 1993. Eddy's mother travelled for four days from Sumatra to visit her beloved son. She travelled via dug-out canoe, ferry, bus, train, rickshaw, mini-taxi, shit truck and finally by foot, all the while carrying a home-cooked meal for Eddy – who shared it with me. I've eaten some wild stuff in my life but this bag of dog's intestines, stuffed with fish paste and pork that had been unrefrigerated for days . . . all I can say is, if you ever see Pruit Angin on a menu, give it a miss.

BELOW: Here I am with some of the Pamakasan Prison guards on Madura Island. As you can see, I was quite free to roam the prison at night with the guards but I couldn't have escaped because they constantly followed me, wanting to talk about what life was like in the West. I didn't know . . . I hadn't been there since I was 19.

ABOVE: This is a photo taken in East Timor in 1983 of Ngadimun (sixth from left), my room boy in Malang Prison, during his service in the Indonesian Army. Ngadimun served in the Indonesian Army for 23 years and did two tours of duty in East Timor. The first one, in 1972, was spent mapping out the internal structure of the Portuguese opposition. Ngadimun, along with the rest of the soldiers, was an unarmed combat expert, trained to kill quite easily without weapons. These were the soldiers responsible for the execution of five Australian journalists. The story was told to me by Ngadimun after he converted to Christianity and confessed all his sins (or at least most of them).

BELOW: This is Block B of Pamakasan Prison during exercise period. Each one of the doors in the background is a cell, less than 180 cm x 180 cm. We all had to do this exercise called 'SKG' or Ess Kar Gee. It is a form of martial arts. As punishment we were made to exercise. It might be a good idea in theory to keep a prisoner fit – but it also makes for some very tough, ruthless bastards who are far from ordinary.

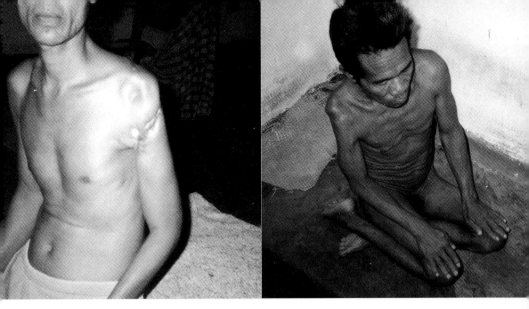

ABOVE LEFT: This prisoner in Pamakasan Prison had been chopped across the arm with a machete. The white spot is cotton wool, which he had to stuff inside a hole in his arm that wouldn't heal and constantly oozed pus. The wound is six months old.

ABOVE RIGHT: This photo was taken in Block B of Pamakasan Prison. The prisoner had not worn clothes for over six years because of some strange skin infection. Wearing clothes or being touched caused him excruciating pain. For the whole time I was in Pamakasan Prison, I heard this guy moaning ceaselessly, pitifully every single night. No one cared if he lived or died . . . even him.

BELOW: This is the front of Pamakasan Prison morgue. They had to post a guard outside the morgue because the prisoners had no qualms about robbing the dead. When alive the prisoners often hid gold chains, rings and cash up their butts. When dead, they were open game for other, still breathing, prisoners. In many cases where one prisoner had killed another it was accepted practice to cut off a piece of your dead enemy and eat it. How hungry you were decided how much you ate. A piece of ear was the most popular trophy.

RIGHT: Four prisoners on Madura Island carry a four-handled box. The box is a very handy item – it acts as a rice carrier at meal times and after the gang fights and riots these food boxes would be used to carry the dead or injured. One box for two jobs shows the Indonesian ingenuity.

BELOW: Suppertime on Madura Island. Everyone liked to be served first because the food boxes were also used to carry bleeding bodies or corpses. If you were served from the bottom of the box, chances were there'd be bits and pieces of questionable odds and ends served up with your food.

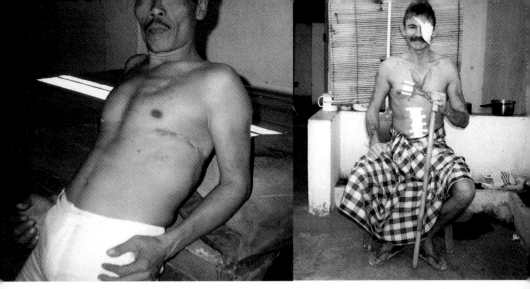

ABOVE LEFT: This is Farta. He was chopped across the shoulder by a prisoner called Jarb. When Jarb pulled out the cleaver from Farta's chest, the gaping hole was so big that Farta's left lung popped out and up, looking like he had just given birth to a new head. Farta was a tough bastard!

ABOVE RIGHT: This is me in Malang Prison 11 days after I was stabbed. A prison guard took this photo, to prove to the Australian Embassy that I was still alive.

BELOW: This photo was taken by my sister Lynette six weeks after I was stabbed. She and her husband, Ken (second from right), came to visit me even though Ken was undergoing treatment for cancer. It was the first time I had seen my sister in over 20 years. Sadly, Ken died not long after this photo was taken. Note: The hockey-shaped stick behind the seated guard was used to hook around prisoners to break up fights. Notice the nails sticking out . . . they hurt! Especially when used around your throat.

ABOVE: Here I am with one of the Islamic fundamentalists in Malang Prison. He was serving 20 years for his involvement in the conspiracy to blow up the Nusa Dua Resort Hotel in Bali. He had just told me that he would happily put bombs around his own mother, daughter or wife if he thought that it would get rid of their President Soeharto and the Golkar Party.

BELOW: This is a blowfly's view of the prisoners' toilet in Pamakasan Prison. It was said within the prison that if a man only shat twice a day, he must have been constipated.

ABOVE: This photo was taken in Block E in Tanggerung Prison in 1995. Three prisoners shared this cell. Many of the prisoners in Tanggerung Prison were members of the Ambon Christian Party. It is pretty much a well-known fact that throughout the Islands of Ambon there are many militant Christian factions prepared and armed for what they see as an inevitable conflict with Islam.

BELOW: This photo was taken in Tanggerung Prison in Jakarta. We were all eating when the guard came in to take our picture. Of course we had to cover the costs for his efforts.

While I was in prison, my family and friends back in Australia never stopped pressuring the Australian government. Thanks to them, a great deal of media coverage helped

mind, the guards were already there and so too was the prison doctor Bawana, along with a couple of the trustee prisoners.

Bawana told them to clean up the floor and wash the walls of the dry caking and congealing blood with some savage-smelling antiseptic. He then started to wash and clean my legs.

It felt like I had been submerged into fire, as he scraped and cleaned away the shit and dirt that had encrusted on the wounds of my legs. As I groaned and tossed he ordered the guards to take off my handcuffs, but having free hands didn't help. It only gave me a better view through my one good eye, of the slabs of skin that he was putting back over my bones and my swollen kneecaps, not to mention the swelling of the old family jewels. My balls had grown to the size of leather-coated custard apples.

That day when Bawana was leaving the cell, he looked down at the bulge of shining skin between my legs and nearly cried as he gave me another shot of morphine.

'I'll try to get back tomorrow at the same time, but if they . . .' he said, nodding at the bulge of cods that were hanging between my legs, 'start to ache, then take these.' He dropped two tablets onto the floor, where I was lying naked.

I nodded straight off to sleep, after the clink, clink, squeak, slam of the cell, and dreamt of a life without hurt.

When I woke up, it was late at night and I was freezing my arse off, my body was aching in places that I didn't even know I had. As I rolled onto one side of my face, I sucked up the two pills that Bawana had left me on the floor. I crunched them down and, within half an hour, I was dead to the world.

When I next awoke, on the fourth day after being recaptured, my body was aching all over. I managed to wiggle to the wall and, as I propped myself up against it, I was amazed. The swelling in my balls had gone down completely. Overnight the little buggers had returned to just about normal.

I was rapt, but the rest of my body still hurt like a bitch. As I was surveying the cell and rechecking my own damage, the block was opened and the guards made their way to the Don's cell. He was taken to the KPLP office for more questions. I hadn't realised it at the time, or the four days that I was in limbo, but the Don and the Chook had been taken daily to the KPLP office for interrogations and beatings. (The only reason that I wasn't taken out was because I had been so badly beaten when I'd been recaptured, the guards were under the opinion that I would die any day.)

They were trying to find out who had arranged the passports and the valid immigration stamp for the Bali international airport that the Don had on his passport, which he had so freely given to the soldiers who picked him up on the beach the week before.

The Don and Chook had been telling different stories about how the Don had got the passport and stamp. But when the Chook's belongings were searched, they found his passport also, which caused them to both have some serious questions thrown at them, not to mention serious punches and kicks.

I was caught with nothing, except a Bible – everything else I pissed off while I was drowning at sea. But the Bible, well, for some odd reason I just couldn't find it inside me to abandon it. After all, it contained $1,300, a passport and an international driver's licence, stashed safely in its covers. If I should have the chance to bolt again, I still had the basic requirements.

The Don held out for over a week, but then he broke down, saying to the Chook, 'I can't take it any more, they beat me enough, I gotta tell them, I gotta tell them, it was Russell who make a the stamps, it was Russell who fix a up the passports, I gotta tell them, I can't a take a no more.'

'I know, I know, don't you think that they bashed me too. We just gotta make up a good story, one the little rice suckers will believe, that's all, mate. Now keep it together and we will work something out. There's no need in giving up Russell, the bastards have beaten him enough. Did you see what they did to his old town halls, mate? The fuckers have done him enough,' the Chook said through the bars.

'But they know,' moaned the Don, 'they know he's here under a false passport. Russell is not his real name, they told me that in the office, they know, they know all about him,' whispered the Dago Dog.

I still couldn't get off the floor after a week. My legs were totally useless. All I could do was drag myself from one corner to the other with my hands.

I managed to crawl my way up to the front bars and said, 'Psss, pssss, hey, Don, can you hear me? I hope you can, because I want you to remember my voice, you spaghetti-sucking slime ball. You think your Italian Wog Mafia is tough? Just give me up, fucker, you just give me up. After I trusted you and tried to help you, you piss on me, and you've made an enemy who will follow you to hell if that's where I have to go.'

'He's OK,' said the Chook from one of the distant cells, 'he's just been bashed a lot. Look, I've got an idea, I can cover us all. Hey Don, don't give up Russ, he's our ace up the sleeve. We need him, you and I can't dress up books like him. Just leave it to me. I've got an idea, OK.'

'OK,' whispered the Wog.

'Hey, Spaggo,' I said, 'don't think I am making empty threats, I am no Mafia fuckwit. I am me, I am full of poison and I am worse then your shit-arsed fucking godfathers. If I hear that you have given me up, you better make sure I am good and dead. Or I'll come after you. And if you try to hide, I know where your family lives in Venice. I've also got your brothers' and sisters' addresses in Rome and Naples. Eventually you'll come out to one of their fuckin' funerals, then I'll get you, that's why the Mafia never moved to Australia. Our code of silence works all the way, right up to the last living member of your fucking family. So remember that, Don, when you go into the KPLP office again. We bastards from Downunder have got our own set of morals and we stick to them.'

I dragged myself away from the bars, leaving the Don in silence, thinking about what I had just said (Christ, I even frightened myself with that speech!).

When the guards took the Don away the next time, he was returned an hour later. Then the guards dragged the Chook out all geared up. From what I could gather from the guards at the time, the Chook had decided to spill his guts. Well, at least that's what the Don told them the Chook wanted to do.

When the Chook returned two hours later, not only did he have his handcuffs off, he was smoking a bloody cigarette. Ah, thinks I, he's pulled something off. My own self-confidence began to climb. As things turned out he spun them a top story about how he had arranged the escape.

He said that one of his mates, Tim Jones, had arranged the passports, but only for him and the Don, and that the entry stamps were *brumbies* (false), also arranged and made by his mate Tim. Chook said that Tim had financed the whole plot, including the cars, and that if Tim Jones ever returned to Indonesia, the Chook would be glad to give evidence against him.

Oh . . . and he added that Russell had no part in the planning of the escape, he only learnt about it on the night that the Don and he (the Chook) were going, and he (Russell) cut out the bars of his own cell and followed. End of story, end of case.

The Don was rapt, so too was everybody else.

For the next three and a half months we were kept in separate cells, with our arms handcuffed behind our backs.

For the first month the guards who were on the shift that we tried to escape from would come in every night they worked and beat us. The reason that they did this was because they were totally pissed off and hated our guts. They had all been demoted and with demotion came a cut in wages.

Most of them were living on less than $60 a month and if you've got a wife and three or four kids to feed, and you want to send your kids to school with clothes on their backs, shoes on their feet and books in their hands, and that $60 is cut down to $50 or $45, naturally you'd get pissed off too (or use your brain and find a better-paying job).

One of their real bad habits was coming in at night with buckets of shit and piss and throwing them over us. They loved throwing the shit on us, it was a big turn on for them. If they could sneak up to your cell and catch you lapping water out of a dirty aluminium dish and cover you in shit, that was a ten-point hit.

As our hands were handcuffed, in order to eat and drink we had to get down on our knees and lap from plates on the floor, like dogs. Once your head was down, and you were on your knees, you were a much easier target.

The first prisoner to risk visiting any of us during that time was old Pak Puji. He would bring his rag and bucket into the block every time he got the chance and start washing the main floor of the block on his hands and knees, lingering around our cells for a quick few words.

Kim and Dave, the two New Zealanders, would slip him notes to pass on to me, along with a handful of vitamin tablets every now and then, and of course he would slip us some of his own special medicine.

When there were no guards around, he would pull out extra food that he had wrapped in plastic bags and stashed in his bucket of dirty greasy water. We would ravenously eat the food, and use the plastic bags to wrap around ourselves at night to stay warm.

Those cells got freezing at night and when the wind blew it got worse. If you think Bali is a warm tropical paradise, then spend the tail end of the monsoon season naked, chained up, bare-arsed in a cell on a wet concrete floor. Saying it's cold would be the understatement of my life (though I've made quite a few of those before).

Kim was my first white visitor. After the first month of solitary in Block C, Kim was given permission to feed us the regular foreigners' food again.

The other blokes who came to see us were few and far between, because if the guards caught them in our block they gave them a toe up the arse and a clip across the lugs for their effort. The only blokes who ever bothered to venture over to say hello and smuggle us in some extra food or cigarettes, or coffee, whenever the chance popped up, were the Kiwis Kim and Dave, Antonio the Spaniard, August the Dutchie and, to my surprise, Musaki, the Japanese prisoner whose cell we escaped through. Musaki took it really well, though in all truth he only came over to see if he could get more downers. But the bulk of the foreign prisoners were too afraid to risk trying to visit us because they didn't want to get involved.

They all feared that the guards might think they were somehow involved in our escape attempt, and that they might lose their remissions. The only Aussies who visited me were John, Andrew the fisherman and Sam, the bloke I had met the night I was transferred to Krobokan Prison.

A couple of Aussie prisoners complained about our treatment to the Australian Embassy and Consulate in Bali.

'There is nothing we can do. Russell and James are convicted drug traffickers and ex-escapees and they're being punished according to Indonesian laws,' the Consulate informed them.

So basically shut up and piss off with your complaints.

However, the International Red Cross took a totally different view of the whole matter when they paid a visit to the prison and discovered what our condition was after three and a half months of solitary in handcuffs.

The Red Cross did occasional spot checks on Pak Puji, the one and only political prisoner. They were one of the few organisations that had the right to check out his living conditions and to visit him in his cell, rather than in a contrived atmosphere like the prison offices or official visiting rooms.

Once when they were in Block C, which Pak Puji generally had to himself, he told them about the three foreign prisoners who were also being held in the block with him. He told them about our beatings and what had been done to us – the same treatment he had suffered nearly 25 years ago. Pak Puji was no man's fool – he spoke to the Red Cross official about us in Dutch. The Dutch bloke from the International Red Cross was also no fool. To cover Pak Puji he insisted on checking out where the toilets were in the block, where the prisoner (Pak Puji) could bath and wash himself, where he could exercise in the block and so forth.

This stuck a burr up the guards' arseholes, especially the KPLP chief Susanta. But I was unaware of all these happenings at the time; all I knew was the guards quickly dashed into my cell, removed the handcuffs, gave me a clean shirt and a pair of shorts to put on, and threw a cane mat down on the floor.

Ten minutes later, a tall grey-haired foreigner appeared at my cell.

'Good morning,' he said. 'Do you speak English?'

'Yes,' I replied.

'Ah, that's very good. I was only told that there were foreigners here, and I wasn't too sure if they spoke English. What is your name?' he said.

'Ah, Russell,' I replied.

'And what is your nationality?' he continued.

Who's this guy? I thought, and how did he get in here? 'Are you a policeman?' I asked.

He smiled as he replied, 'No, no, I am not a policeman, my name is Gustoff, Dr Gustoff. I am a representative of the International Red Cross.' He poked a thick pink arm through the cell bars, offering me his hand.

I reached out to shake it, and his hand was so big that mine seemed to vanish in the palm of his, with the ends of my fingers barely sticking out the other side.

'Gee, you've got big hands,' I said, which I suppose was a pretty silly thing to say, but then I added to it by saying, 'I bet you don't specialise in microsurgery.'

His smile grew. But when he looked down at his huge hands encompassing mine it quickly faded, then softened as his eyes focused on my wrists.

'How long have they kept you in shackles?' he asked as he held up my hand and examined it.

'Nearly three and a half months now,' I replied, as I looked at the damaged wrists at the end of my arms. Those three-and-a-half months of handcuffs had taken their toll. My left wrist had two big oozing ulcers. My right was callused in places and skinless in others.

'But Pak Puji has been giving me medicine to help stop the infection,' I said.

'What man does to man,' he sighed, as Susanta came up beside him.

'How long has this man been held in shackles?' Dr Gustoff snapped with contempt. His whole attitude changed towards Susanta.

'We don't use shackles in this prison,' Susanta said, indignantly.

'No, they use handcuffs,' I said. 'That's what they use and that's what I had on half an hour ago, and that's what I've been in for the past three-and-a-half months: handcuffs.'

'That's a lie,' Susanta yelled. 'This prisoner is no concern of yours, he is a troublemaker and he tried to escape. He is a drug addict, don't believe anything he tells you.'

'I am not blind, Mr Susanta, and I am not a fool. I've seen shackle marks on people in Africa and South America, but this is the first time I've seen them here in Indonesia, and I will report it,' Dr Gustoff said.

So then he went about what the International Red Cross is all about. He called over his three friends, one of whom was a very thick-thighed lady in her early fifties, who washed, cleaned then bandaged my wrists, gave me a tetanus injection and a course of antibiotics.

Dr Gustoff asked several questions and when I told him that my embassy knew about me being held in handcuffs and had done nothing about it, he was shocked.

He couldn't believe that they had not put up some sort of official complaint or protest to the Indonesian government about our treatment.

The Red Cross representatives also checked out the Chook and the Don. One of them, who could speak Italian, was horrified at what the guards had done to Guiseppe's face.

When the Red Cross finally left the block we were held in, I was feeling on top of the world, but about two hours later the guards turned up. All our cells were unlocked and they came in swinging.

They beat the shit out of the three of us and our handcuffs were replaced, but not for long. Three days later, they were removed and we were all thrown into one cell.

So it seems that where the Australian Embassy, and the Italian Embassy for that matter, didn't want to get involved in Indonesia's judicial penal affairs, the Red Cross did. God bless the Red Cross!

CHAPTER 9

THE VOMIT COMET

Death to me is really no worry
It comes to us all
I suppose it must be like
God tapping you on the shoulders and saying
'OK, arsehole, your time's up, out of the pool'

I really wish that I were literate enough to describe on paper what it felt like when those handcuffs were taken off after three and a half months. My hands were so used to being together that they just seemed to naturally come together, whether it be behind my back or in front of me, for well over a month after they were removed. But I suppose it's something you would have to experience to really understand.

Five months after the escape bid, the Chook, the Don, John and myself were all tranferred out of Krobokan Prison.

Eight of us (all in chains) were crammed into a small minibus, about the size of a Volkswagen Campervan. The front of the van was closed off for the driver, his co-driver and one of the policemen, who was by law supposed to accompany all prisoners during transfer.

The back of the van was also enclosed so as to accommodate two more policemen with rifles and a KPLP security prison guard. The area that they had in the van was the same as we eight prisoners had. It was impossible for us all to sit down on the small wooden benches that were built into the tiny prison van. Six of us sat on the two side benches while the other two lay on the floor. Because the conditions were so tight, two prisoners on each bench were forced to sit with their backs against the van wall, while the bloke in the middle sat forward, right on the edge of the bench, thus belting his head constantly against the head of the prisoner perched up on the opposite seat. We had to rotate our positions, so that everyone got a chance to stretch his legs on the floor and sit up at the front of the cab to breathe some fresh air, from the two small vents on either side of the van's side walls.

It took just on 12 hours to get to Surabaya on Java. During that time if you wanted a piss, you had to piss on the floor, which was a bummer for the two blokes whose turn it was to lay there.

Then of course there were the two spewers who suffered from motion sickness and every hour spewed their guts up. I eventually nicknamed the van 'The Vomit Comet'.

Eight men in an airless jolting, spew- and piss-ridden box, with an area no more than what you'd find in the confines of four or five coffins – but we were lucky. That same month, 33 prisoners were transferred from Kalimantan to Madura, eight of whom died from suffocation while being transported.

When we arrived at Kali Sosok Prison in Surabaya, we oozed out of the transport van and were lined up against a wall and hosed down, to wash the shit, vomit, dirt and piss off us. We were all extremely happy little vegemites, and I guess that's just what we all looked like we'd been covered in. I suspect that they only gave us a quick hose down to see which ones were the white ones.

Kali Sosok was a pretty hard prison, with a capacity of over 7,000 prisoners. During my short stay of just a couple of weeks, I soon realised I had to constantly stay on my toes, because of the murder of one of the prison guards. The guard had worked in the prison kitchen and after an argument, which he lost, he ended up in one of the huge rice steamers. He stayed there from 4 p.m. in the afternoon until 4.30 a.m. the following morning.

When the prisoners who put him in the steamer tried to pull him out the following morning, he virtually dissolved in their hands. The meat was steamed off the bones, like that of an over-cooked chicken. His cooked flesh was a greyish colour, with a spiteful odour about it. To get rid of this steamed corpse, the prisoners broke the flesh up into small portions, then equally distributed little pieces to as many of the 3,000 to 5,000 prisoners as possible. All of the bones were then crushed up and scattered around the prison yards, or fed to cats or rats.

When the kitchen was eventually searched by the guards looking for their missing workmate, all they found of him were parts of his boiled uniform and some buttons, along with his skull and his hip bone, which the lads in the kitchen hadn't had time to crush up.

Your choices were very limited.

You were either with them, or you were against them.

If being against them meant you could end up in a fucking big rice steamer, then I'd happily choose to be with them. I was content to pick my teeth and comfortably fart along with the other survivors.

After a few weeks, the Chook, the Don and I had to say our goodbyes to John in Kali Sosok Prison as we three ex-escapees were sent on to Madura Island, where one of Indonesia's most infamous punishment prisons was situated. That is where we were told that we would either finish our sentences, or die.

Parmakasan Prison is where they send Indonesia's hard-core prisoners. The mass murderers, the sadistic murderers, the uncontrollable homicidals, the necrophiliacs, the cop killers, the lowly child molesters, the prisoners who kill too many other inmates in other prisons and, of course, the worst of them all, ex-escapees. All in all, the prison consisted of about 80 per cent murderers.

At least I knew where I stood. We spent the first few months in the RS, or Ruma Sakit, which is a kind of prison infirmary-cum-leper block. The prison had such a high death rate that it had two morgues to handle the bodies. As fast as the prisoners went out under sheets they would be replaced with those from other prisons.

Whereas most of the guards in Krobokan Prison could speak English, even if only a few words, and I had been able to speak a little Balinese mixed with Indonesian, things were very different in Parmakasan Prison. Here they spoke Maduranese mixed with Javanese and Indonesian.

It didn't take long to realise we'd need an interpreter.

That interpreter appeared in the form of Barry, an Aussie bloke who had spent the past three years on Madura Island on his own in the prison. He was serving a nine-year sentence for hashish and he had tried to escape from Krobokan Prison three years earlier. He really wasn't such a bad bloke, but Christ he was bent – but then again, so too was Madura. Barry couldn't speak a full sentence in English without using Maduranese or Indonesian.

If I were to write down all the stories from Parmakasan Prison, there is no way any sane person could possibly believe them. That is, of course, unless that person had been a prisoner there, or one of the guards.

There was, for starters, the *incident* in the kitchen.

One of the prisoners had gone *pusing*, because his wife wanted to go to Egypt to work as a servant girl in some rich Arab's house. (Pusing in Indonesia can mean to be stressed, upset, confused, angry, dizzy, drunk, to have a headache or to be pissed off – this guy fell into all of the above). This prisoner, whose name was Jarb, didn't want his wife to go overseas, but when he heard that she had gone, he got seriously pusing.

The next day, a meat day, Jarb's emotions surfaced. I mention that it was a meat day simply because it's only twice a week that the prisoners in Indonesian prisons are fed meat.

Prisoners are supposed to be given 65 grams of meat each, but if they get

10 grams then they're very lucky bastards indeed, especially in a punishment prison such as Parmakasan.

The prison kitchen workers were expected to cut the meat off the bones so the guards could take the meat home, then the bones were cut and cracked up and fed to the prisoners. (Keep in mind that when a guard is earning $60 each month, and a kilo of meat costs $3 to $4, his family doesn't see a lot of meat, not when a kilo of the stuff costs him well over a day's wages.)

As the guards were coming in to collect their meat, with the prison corruption flowing at its peak, Jarb flipped out and started to hack up the other prisoners with his meat cleaver. He cut one prisoner across the forehead and the bloke's face just dropped away in a fold of skin and pouring blood.

He hacked down on the shoulder of Farta, who was the kitchen prison boss, and when he pulled the cleaver up and out of Farta's shoulder, Farta's lung popped up and out, looking like he was giving birth to a new head.

Jarb then leapt at another prisoner who held up his hands to protect his face, but as the cleaver chopped down, it chopped off four of his fingers as cleanly as if they were twigs.

One of the old guards, a bloke who had less than six months before he was to be pensioned off, stepped in front of Jarb. Jarb slashed across sideways, cutting right through the old bastard's uniform and right through his rib cage.

I was the first to hit the wall and run up it. The wall that I am referring to is the one that ran around the kitchen to keep out the hungry prisoners it was supposed to feed. It was about two-and-a-half metres tall and, with Jarb running around with that fucking chopper, I was really truly inspired to reach the top of that wall in one go.

I wasn't alone on the wall for long. The other prisoners took my lead, and soon enough we were all perched up on top, watching Jarb chopping away at the slower prisoners.

The last and slowest was Allie, the prisoner who was first chopped across the forehead while sleeping in one of the rice trays-cum-body boxes. Allie had a horrible handicap. He was trying to run while holding up his face. The way he had been cut, his eyebrows and forehead skin kept falling onto his face, along with a heap of blood, and I'm sure you know how head wounds bleed. He couldn't see all that well and seemed to be just running around in circles, until Jarb caught up with him from behind.

Grabbing Allie's hair from the back, he pulled him to the ground. With three large swings from his strong arms and both hands on the handle of the chopper, Jarb hacked off Allie's head, then stood up holding the head in his left hand and the chopper in his right. The atmosphere was that of a primal arena, a barbarian's killing ground.

If nothing else, that Jarb was pretty nifty with that bloody cleaver. He sure had a good eye for the chop.

When the freaked-out guards finally got their shit together and shot Jarb three times, killing the crazy fuck, there were two dead, two mortally injured and three others badly cut, including one spaced-out case with a bag of fingers who was asking the guards if the police could take them off his record.

'See, I am not using them. See, they're in the bag. They're not mine. Someone else has been using them. I want a new trial. I am innocent. I didn't kill those girls. They're not my fingers. See, how can they be? They're not on me. I am clean. I am clean, ha ha ha. Watch those fingers. Send them to the police, ha ha ha. I am going home. They're not my fingers.' Off he went, holding a bleeding stump.

During the couple of months that I was in the leper block, or the RS, I had gained the friendship of some flaky friends; they were both lepers and life wasn't treating them well. Some days they just seemed to fall apart over nothing.

They both had dry leprosy and I made the occasional joke to the Don about having flaky friends, but he either didn't pick up on it, or he closed his ears.

The worst fight I've ever seen in my life, was on the day we were moved out of the RS.

My two leper mates had a blue over some soap, and a few odds and ends, which I had left behind telling them to share the stuff between them.

When they first started to scuffle, the Chook and I thought that it was kind of funny, but as they started to well and truly beat the shit out of each other, and their bandages all started to come undone and fall off, I realised that some of those bandages were still full.

'Christ Almighty,' I said to the Chook. 'That fucking bandage has still got lumps in it.'

'Yeah,' he replied as the blood drained from his face, 'and that sock that just flew through the air and hit me on the chest, has still got fucking toes in it. These two lipless wonders are fucking tearing each other apart.'

'Then get in there and stop them before they do some serious damage to each other,' I said.

'You're fucking joking,' the Chook replied, 'The bastards might touch me, or worse still, I might touch them.'

So as the bandages flew, and arms and legs waved and wobbled in a dozen different directions, bits and pieces of skin and hair, and the odd tooth fluttered to the ground, Chook and I made our hasty exit from the RS on Madura to our new cells in Block Pusat.

We spent the next few months trying to adjust. Jarb had only recently done his thing when we were called up to the office and told that none of us was now allowed to work, because the prison authorities said that as foreigners, they didn't want us staying for long periods of time where we could be killed, in case one of the prisoners went pusing.

So we didn't have to work, which suited the Chook and me just fine, and we still had the run of the prison.

We could still use the kitchen to do our own cooking and we could still go in and out of the prison workshops. We also had free access to the prison infirmary and the RS, not to mention Block F, which was the Communist Block, where they kept eight little old men who were once members of the PKI, just like old Pak Puji.

In fact all of the blokes in Block F either knew Pak Puji personally or had heard of him. I learned that old Pak Puji was a very big man in his day, but I somehow always knew that he was once a man to be reckoned with. He just had that aura about him and I am sure that if things had been different in Indonesia in the 1960s, Pak Puji would have become a man of importance, not only in Indonesia but on the world stage.

Pak Puji wasn't really a communist, he was a union boss, and if that was, or is what a communist is, then my father would have been in prison long before I was born, because he was always a union man. He was a painter and docker, and his own personal philosophy on life was, 'When you're small, be strong, and when you're strong, remember the small.'

So if that is what communism is all about, then I suppose I am a commie too, because I really believe, with all the heart and soul that I now possess as an older man in the middle of his life, that if we're strong, we should remember the weak.

Are they the words of a communist, a capitalist, a Buddhist, a Christian, or maybe a fool?

It's better that you decide, for I am only writing these words. You're the one who is reading them . . .

As the first year passed, I started to discover the meaning of the word boredom, and to relieve myself of it, I spent hours with my guitar picking and plucking.

When I discovered the chords that sung out F U C K K K K K W I T, I thought: that sounds like Fuckwit. I played it again, and realised that was just what that Gat had said or played.

I finally threw the guitar down on the floor of my piss-arsed shit box cell and headed off looking for mischief, wherever I could find it.

The Chook was my first target.

I found an old green woollen sock, with holes in the toes and the heel, lying on the ground outside one of the guard's towers. I picked it up and headed for the Chook's cell, intending to stick it under his pillow.

As I passed the woodwork shop, I was called in by one of the guards to check out a birdcage that he had got the prisoners to make for his wife.

'I bet you don't have birdcages in Australia like this,' he proudly said, pointing at the birdcage.

The guard was still talking, asking me questions and answering them himself, when I noticed an empty nail box. I picked it up and filled it with sawdust, then I stood up and started to leave.

As I looked at the guard I could hear the strings of my guitar play F U C K K K K K W I T.

'So what do you think? What do you think of my cage?' he asked in Maduranese.

'Fuckwit,' I replied in English.

'Yeah, I knew that you would like it,' he said in Maduranese. 'Do you think my wife will like it?' he continued.

'It's hard to say,' I said speaking in Maduranese. 'Do you think she will fit inside?' I patted him on the back and said, 'It won't fit her, the turd tray isn't big enough.' I left the woodwork shop, feeling good.

When I arrived at the Chook's cell, or slot as we used to sometimes call them, he was playing Seven Scop, a card game, with a couple of child molesters and a priest killer.

I walked past them and went into my cell, pulled out the daggy sock and the empty nail carton filled with sawdust and made up a pretty little present.

When I walked back into Chook's cell, everyone was still engrossed in the card game.

'Hey, Chook! I was asked to give this to you,' I said, as I held out the little box.

'Ah, I love presents,' he said as he opened it up, giving it a shake.

When he ripped off the paper and found the box, he opened it and, brushing off the sawdust, pulled out the crusty green sock.

'What the fuck is this?' he said, holding up the sock.

'Try it on, it's from your old mate,' I replied, but he couldn't hear me through the laughter from the other prisoners.

'A fucking sock. Hey, look boys, I've got a sock for a present and only one,' the Chook said.

'Try it on, try it on,' cried one of the child molesters, followed by a chorus of, 'Try it on, try it on, try it on.'

The Chook pulled it on. To the claps and cheers of everyone he held up his sock-clad foot, with half his toes sticking out, and said, 'And who the fuck sends me one rotten sock?'

'No Toes,' I replied.

'Who?' he asked.

'No Toes, that's his sock, he asked me to give it to you. He doesn't need it any more, he's lost his feet now,' I said, as the Chook's eyes flung up, and he started to savagely pull the sock off his foot.

No Toes was one of the lepers who had the fight in the RS the day we were moved. His sock had hit the Chook in the chest and at the time, it still had toes in it. That's why we nicknamed him No Toes.

When I next saw the Chook, he was bent over the well, desperately pulling up buckets of water and flushing his feet. Then he squatted down with a coarse black brush used to scrub out the moss and fungus in the mandi, or bathing troughs, and started to scrub the skin off his left foot.

For the next week I avoided the Chook.

My next victim was the Don.

I called him into my cell one very hot and humid day. He had just finished working in his garden and the sweat was pouring out from all over his sun-baked brown body.

'Hey Don, I've just scored some ice.' (Ice was a luxury in the prison.) 'Come and have a cold drink,' I said.

When he came into the cell all smiles, he squatted down on the floor beside the Chook and said, 'She's a hotta than a whore's a snatch outta side.'

'Too right,' replied the Chook, as he passed the Don his icy cold plastic mug of pineapple juice.

The Don had a big swig and passed the mug back to the Chook saying, 'Ah, thatta she tastes a beautiful.'

'Here,' I said, giving him a clean empty mug, 'Help yourself.' I pointed to the tea kettle that was used for everything from boiling water to cooking stews, to holding ice juice.

The Don poured himself a drink and we spent the next half hour gum-flapping.

When the Don had finished his mug he refilled it, sat back down and we started to discuss the finer points of growing tomatoes, turning a chick on, rolling joints, how to fix the pulley over the well, how good it was to have a nice cold icy drink on a hot day and how nipples are so important in lovemaking, not to mention which guard was the greatest arsehole, which prisoner was the most bent, which cars we thought were the best, how you can tell when bananas are ripe, and how's the best way of pulling leeches off you when their attached to your balls.

We basically talked prison shit.

When the Don got up again from the floor he went and picked up the kettle; after topping up mine and the Chook's mugs, he started to refill his own. While he was pouring, the stem of the kettle suddenly blocked up, so he gave it a quick swish around and tried again.

The juice poured out a little then the kettle's stem blocked up again.

'Something inside no wanna the juice to flow,' he said, then took the kettle's top off to check out what was inside blocking the flow of juice.

When he looked into it, his brow wrinkled up in a questioning way, 'Hey whatta this?' he said, as his hand went into the open kettle, pulling out a crunched up soggy gray cloth, all speckled in bits of pineapple.

'Ah, it's just what I used to filter out the big bits. But it fell back into the kettle so I thought fuck it, and left it inside,' I answered.

As the Don started to unfold the grey rag, his eyes lit up.

'Porca Dia,' he screamed, as he flung the rag from his hand.

'Porca Madonna, they're your fucking underpants. You're a crazy fuck, you sick, you sick, in the head,' he yelled, poking a finger at his temple with his eyes bulging from his head.

The Chook leapt off the floor, checked out the underpants that now lay spread open on the deck.

'Christ, they are your underpants. Couldn't you have found something bloody better to strain the pineapples with?' he asked.

'Well I would have used No Toes' sock, only you burned the bastard,' I replied.

The Chook went white, nearly as white as the Don had turned, and then his shoulders gave a little shudder.

'Did you wash them first?' the Chook asked.

'Of course I did, what do you think I am, a dirty bastard or something? I washed them last week when we all did our washing, remember?' I said, as I started getting all stroppy about it.

'Oh well, that's OK. Shit, for a moment there, I thought they were dirty,' he replied.

'Jesus Kristus, they no only wanna 12 years of my life to spend in the bloody prison, but they wanna me to spend it in a crazy house, with the crazy people. Porca Madonna,' the Don said, then stormed out of my cell, refusing to talk to me for nearly two months.

When the Don had gone, the Chook picked up his mug, looked inside it then over at me saying, 'You really did wash those baggy-arsed Y-fronts last week, didn't you?'

'Sure I did, you were there, remember?' I said.

'Yeah, yeah, that's right I remember,' he said with a smile, then finished drinking his mug of pineapple juice and passed the empty mug over to me.

Still smiling he said, 'I'd drink anything strained through anything, except for No Toes' fuckin' socks.' He left the cell laughing.

'You're bent,' I yelled at him. 'What's the matter with No Toes' socks?'

My next victim was the prison's head of security (or the KPLP), Mr Bartak.

Naturally I had to start slow with him, to feel out the waters so to speak.

I made a request to see him one morning and was taken to his office, which reminded me of a tool shed – and not a very modern one at that. On either side of his office ran other offices, all side by side, and all the prison offices were built against the front wall of the prison.

Bartak's office had lower windows set into the wall, and they were the first thing that struck me. They were louvres, so easily removed. Now that's a good exit point, I thought, and a plan was starting to formulate in my mind.

The walls in Parmakasan Prison had electric wires running around the tops of them, unlike Krobokan Prison, which only had barbed wire and broken glass. So if I were to go over the wall here, there was a chance that I would end up suffering the same fate as one of the prisoners who had tried it and was found the next morning, far from happy.

He was actually dead and the guards left him hanging off the wall for most of that day, mainly because the police, some doctors, a couple of blokes from the Justice Department and a couple of prisons officers had to check out the body and its position, but also so that the other prisoners could get a good look and take the warning: Don't try to escape.

The Chook and I interpreted the warning more as: Don't try the wall, that is of course unless you're wrapped in rubber, or you try it when there is a blackout (which were very common on Madura).

But the louvres in Bartak's office caught my eye. All I had to do was somehow get into his office, either day or night, but the time had to be right. The Chook and I put our heads together and planned another escape – we just had to bide our time.

The prison on Madura was so poor, mainly because of the corruption there, that when things broke they either stayed broken or were repaired in the cheapest way.

The Dutch had built the prison in 1912 and it was very primitive. There were no taps in the prison, only wells, with one or two hand pumps that sometimes worked. There were no toilets, only open drains where the prisoners had to squat to relieve themselves.

A good 80 per cent of the prisoners suffered from constant dysentery, or diarrhoea. If you only shat once a day you were classed as constipated. The average prisoner dropped his guts two, three or four times a day. We all suffered fear of farting and wet farts were a real bummer (that's one of my drier jokes, get it?). The prisoners were shitting themselves faster than their bodies could properly digest the miserable amounts of food they ate.

Having a shit was pretty deadly because of the rats. The bastards were nearly as big as the prison cats, only much braver, and they lived quite happy and healthy in the drains eating shit.

After you had a shit and checked it out, which is something we all do, you could always notice bits of beans, still green, bits of corn or carrot all still glowing with their natural colour. A bit crunched up and chewed maybe, but still basically as good as when you first ate them and that's what the rats hoed into.

All shit was a top tasty hot meal to them, the greedy little bastards. Actually I was quite fascinated at times to watch them run up and down the shit drains, then suddenly stop, bury their noses into a turd and pull out a piece of what they considered tasty. I often wondered how they knew that little piece of munchy was in there – they must have had an incredible sense of smell.

The real problem was, once or twice a month, the prisoners on the punishment detail would have to clean out the growing mounds of shit. They'd start flushing and washing it out of the prison through a number of sewerage and sullage grates firmly cemented into the prison walls. All these sewerage outlets led to a small creek that passed by the outside of the prison.

On the opposite side of this creek was a pasar, or market, where the villagers swam, bathed and washed their wares, such as vegetables, to make them look more appetising to their would-be customers.

Cleaning out these shit drains was an experience all of its own as the rats came out in force to protect their homes, their young ones and their stash of shit.

These days I regard it as the Battle of the Bilge and I am sure that the rats had better tacticians on their side. The big bastards would fake a frontal or side attack and when you thought that you had them on the run, out of nowhere another battalion of the bludgers would charge from another drain or down from the roofs.

The worst thing you could ever do on these drain-cleaning days, apart from being there, was to wear a sarong or baggy long pants, because the rats could run up them, not on the outside, but up the inside, and savage you badly with their teeth and claws. Those teeth and claws were a far cry from being clean. Infections were rampant and the bite of a rat, whose staple diet is shit, is not a good bite to have.

Needless to say once the Battle of the Bilge was finished, the rats infested the prison even more, looking for food. The prison cats all seemed to go into hiding around this time, except for two and those two cats were mean fuckers.

One was named Londo. He was a pure white cat with blue eyes and no tail and he had balls with a capital B: two big pink buggers that just hung from his arse like big weather-beaten medals some old war veteran proudly wears. No one fucked with Londo – not only did the rats sidestep him, but so too did the bulk of the prisoners.

The other cat was Sheeba. She made Londo look like Tweety Pie. Sheeba was either pregnant, or feeding her new kittens that she would hide all over the prison. When one of Sheeba's kittens was sick or whining too much, or if she was just feeling hungry, she would eat the little bugger. Believe me, I saw it with my own eyes. She really wasn't a very understanding mother.

Together Londo and Sheeba were a pretty formidable team.

I remember one day when the drains were flushed out and the rats were gaining the upper hand, four prisoners had bolted from the drains with bite marks, followed by nearly a dozen of their mates pretending that they were only leaving the battle area to check on their friends' injuries. The rats were fighting better than normal that day.

They must have had a General MacArthur in their midst. With all honesty, I've never seen so many rats before in my life and they were climbing out of the gutters and drains in droves. They were running and dashing all over the block and attacking the prisoners on the punishment details, who were jumping and hopping, kicking and screaming all over the yard of Block A.

'Christ, I would bet my arsehole on a gold chain that the Pied Piper couldn't control this lot,' the Chook said, and he was right.

But Londo and Sheeba could. Man, you should have seen those rats piss off once those two cats dropped in amongst them.

Londo just killed them, as quick as he could catch them, then he just spat them out. Sheeba mauled them, leaving them torn and broken, but still alive, until she found the fattest one, then she'd split to eat it.

As quickly as the rats had come they vanished, back down the drains, with Londo in hot pursuit.

'Now that's one mean cat,' the Chook said with a gleam in his eye. 'My Mum would love him.'

'Why? Have you got a bad case of rats at home?' I asked.

'Yeah,' he replied, 'they came every week to collect the bills.'

Once the drains were cleaned, the rats were hungry and they searched for other food while doing their best to avoid Londo or Sheeba, until there was enough shit in the drains to support them again.

This was a pretty bad time in the prison for someone wanting a shit because you couldn't go alone, you had to get someone to go with you.

The reason for this was because the moment you dropped your pants to have a splash, and that's what we always had, a splash, we shat like water. It was never hard, always soft and sloppy, with the occasional few lumps. I suppose you could say we never had our shit together.

Those rats would hear you coming a mile off and once you hung your arse over the drain they would scamper out at full pelt, all wanting to be first in on the hot turd tucker. The rats were so greedy they wouldn't give you enough time to have your shit and piss off. They ended up leaping up and trying to pull the shit from your arsehole as fast as you were splashing it all over the rest of their mates. So naturally they would end up biting you on the arse, sinking their disease-encrusted teeth into your buttocks, balls and all other exposed lower areas.

That's why you needed a mate to go with you for a shit. You'd both carry sticks and one would stay on guard at one side of the drain, while the bloke having a shit kept his eyes peeled on the opposite side, holding up a stick ready to beat the rats off or keep them at bay. While he dropped his guts.

All in all it was a fairly effective method. That is, of course, unless you had to guard over Barry, or the 'Plague' as he was nicknamed.

Once I can remember chasing the rats back with a stick, as the Plague squatted down for a shit and the smell that came from the bloke – my God. I thought: what does this man eat? Tears poured from my eyes, sweat burst from my skin and I became giddy; my legs were like rubber trying to support me.

Splash, fart, fart, fart, blurppp, wee, wee, squeak, splash, blurpp, fart. The sounds that he was making were staggering.

'I think I just killed one,' he screamed in joy. 'It's not moving, I think it's dead.'

This statement was followed by another grunt and blurp, splats, fart, fart, wee, and the sound of God's forgotten beings pouring out via some hellish thundering bowel pipes.

When he washed his arse and bounced out all smiling in a merry stride, I caught a quick glimpse of what he had left behind for the rats' breakfast. It was a nightmare, the air was so thick I could taste it. I nearly started to spew on the spot.

'By Christ, Plague,' I said, when we were both outside, well away from the closed-in section of the drains, where the prisoners of that block were supposed to have their shits next. 'You've got to see a doctor. Something has crawled up your arse and died,' I gasped, as I started to vomit.

When I finally stopped spewing, I was sitting on one of the cement runways that led to the shitter. When I looked up there were three local prisoners standing over me, one of whom was holding a bucket of water to wash his arse, while the other two were holding sticks.

'Lots of rats?' the bloke with the bucket of water asked.

'Worse, much worse,' I said.

'What's worse than the rats?' asked one of the prisoners, who was holding a stick.

'Barry,' I answered, and with that they looked at each other with knowing glances and headed for a another shitter. OK, Plague, I thought, when I finish with Bartak, you'll be my next victim.

When my first request to see the KPLP Chief Bartak was granted, I entered his office, sat down on a rickety old chair and gave him my best imbecile smile.

'So what do you want to see me about, Russell?' he asked.

'Chickens, Pak, I'd like to breed some chickens. Pak Mujiano in Block F [which was the subversive block or the Communist block in the prison], he's agreed to help me breed some fighting cocks, but he doesn't have the capital to buy a good new rooster. Pak Mujiano told me about your great loss last month with Akbar, he told me about all its wins in the cockfights. Such a magnificent bird, what a rotten way to go,' I said.

'Yes, yes, you're right, Akbar was a magnificent bird. There's not many like him,' he replied, as he picked up a huge framed photo from his desk and started to stare at it. His hard face softened and he looked like a man who had lost a truly dearly beloved.

'Never lost a fight. Pak Mujiano said that he had had over 100 of them,' I said.

'A hundred and fourteen and probably more. Such a handsome bird he was, as quick as a cobra, only more deadly. Such a beautiful bird,' he said, in the most reverent of voices.

We sat in his office for a good ten minutes of silence and respect as I checked the place over, especially those open louvres. He got all misty-eyed studying the big 12 x 10-inch framed photo of Akbar, that he always kept on his desk, along with the smaller 6 x 4-inch framed photo of his two wives and nine children. The family photo was in black and white, while the one of Akbar was in colour.

The man had his own strange sense of values and priorities. As you've probably gathered, Akbar was a chook, well, not just a chook, he was a fighting cock that had never been defeated in over 100 fights. When a cock loses in a fight, 99 per cent of the time it ends up dead, but Akbar ended his life in a sad way.

He had won three fights in one day with only a scratch, killing his opponents and winning Bartak nearly two months' wages. Bartak was so happy at his good fortune that he went out to celebrate with his cock Akbar in its woven bamboo cage.

As things turned out, he got as drunk as a skunk and so too did the cock. In the open-air night-stall restaurant where Bartak was getting turpsed up, along with his mates, he kept pulling the fighting cock out of its flimsy cage, patting it and forcing down its throat hunks of meat, which he had dipped into his glass of arak (which can get you blotto if you only smell it, let alone drink the shit).

So both Bartak and Akbar ended up out of their trees.

Bets got passed around and a cockfight started in the night market. Akbar would take on all comers and, as drunk as he was, he cleaned up all the local village chooks.

By the end of the night, Bartak's pockets were full of rupees, he had enough money that day to buy himself a new motorcycle, which in Indonesia is big bickies.

When the night markets closed, Bartak staggered off with Akbar in his cage crowing, 'Cock a doodle do, cock a doodle do, any cock will do, and if any of you cocks are game enough, I'll rip off your heads and piss in the sockets.'

Akbar was drunk that night, but he wasn't Robinson Crusoe. Bartak was faced, he fell down in the gutter just outside his house, falling on top of Akbar and killing the cocky bastard.

It was this sad death that Bartak was still getting over that morning when I appeared in his office.

So, I was given permission to breed fighting cocks.

I spent every penny that my family sent me that month to buy one small chicken, the little bastard cost me $A120 and it was only four months old, but old Pak Mujiano loved it, and so too did Bartak. Every chance I got, I would go into the KPLP office to see Bartak, the boss, and report on the chicken's progress.

One morning I caught Bartak just as he had finished the roll call for the morning guards. They were lined up in rows, all 49 of them, not counting the office staff.

When there was a guard's roll call in front of the prison offices, everyone not involved had to stand completely still. To get from one set of blocks to another meant that we had to pass by the prison offices.

We had to either stand still where we were when the first bells rang, or about face and return to where we had just been and wait until the roll call was finished. But we were never allowed to just walk past them during this ceremony, as we were told it showed no respect.

The Chook was with me this particular morning and as he was about to do the 'about turn and piss off', I said, 'Don't leave so soon, better things are about to happen.'

'And what's that?' he asked.

'Stick around and see,' I said.

When all the guards were dismissed and started heading off to the watchtowers, workshops and various prison blocks or wherever, I called out, 'Pak, Pak, Pak Bartak, permissi Pak.'

When he looked around and caught sight of me, his stern face softened.

'Ah, Russell, is there a problem?' he asked.

'Oh no Pak, I just want your advice. You're much more experienced about these things than me,' I replied. 'I am still only learning,' I continued, as I started to walk over towards him with the Chook following behind.

'Well, if I can help you in any way, that's why I am here, to help and

HELL'S PRISONER

advise,' he replied, now piously smiling as though he had just disclosed some lost and forgotten secret to some lost and forgotten son.

'It's about Akbar II. Pak Mujiano says that he should always lift his tail when he has a shit, like all the great fighting cocks. Is that really true?' I asked.

'Yes, that's right, the reason that they lift up their tail is so that they don't shit on their tail feathers, or on their spurs. After all, the male of all species are always cleaner than the females,' he stated, with the look of an intellectual camel on his dial.

'Well, Akbar II does that all the time,' I said. 'But what I am really worried about is his shits – I don't think he's digesting his food properly. Look at this,' and I pulled out an empty cigarette pack that I had half filled with chicken shit, originally destined for a pot plant that I had in my cell.

'Feel this, Pak,' I said, as I pulled out a pinch of chicken shit from the ciggie pack and placed it in his hand. 'Well, maybe I am not an expert, but if any of the cock breeders in Thailand or India were to be holding that, they would start to worry,' I said, as I emptied the pack of chicken shit into his upturned hand.

He just stood there with his hand opened when I dropped the first pinch of chicken shit into it. But when I emptied the lot into it, he lifted up his head to look me in the eye. I could see his mood changing.

Ooooppppppsssss, you've pushed it too far this time, I thought.

'Look, Pak, look,' I said, picking out a piece of shit. 'The colour's all wrong, there's not enough fibre in it and look what happens when I squeeze it: it falls apart. No wonder Indonesia doesn't have any internationally famous cocks, just smell it,' I said, as I held the little piece of chicken shit up to my nose. 'Empty,' I said. 'It's got no fight in it.'

That's when Bartak's face changed for the 68th time, from one of the fatherly figure, to shock, to kill the little bastard, and finally to, hey, the little prick knows.

'Is this how they pick a good fighting cock in other countries?' Bartak asked, holding up a handful of shit.

'Of course, Pak,' I replied, as if everyone in the world were aware of the answer.

'Isn't that how you pick a cock in Indonesia?' I said.

'Well, well, yes, though we do have the traditional method, but this is very interesting. Yes, well I'll just look into it,' he said, as he picked up a small turd from his hand and crumpled it up between his thumb and finger, smelling it.

'Yes, yes, the idea is very sound,' he continued, as he turned away, heading to his office with one handful of chicken shit, studying it as though he was on the verge of discovering the mysteries of the world and didn't want anyone to disturb him.

'You're fucking twisted, but as an ex-car salesman, if I ever open up a used car sales lot, please come and work with me. You were fucking terrific, you made a handful of shit look like gold. Christ, you nearly had me sticking my fingers in it to check the shit out too. Man I thought that he was going to start tasting it – he only needed the slightest nudge,' the Chook said, as we headed back to our own block.

'Yeah, that was the plan, but I don't want to push him too fast. I bet I can get him eating chicken shit before the month's out,' I said, and we both burst into laughter.

After that I used to enjoy watching Bartak wander around F Block when he was there to check out the cocks. He'd pick up bits of chicken shit, wet or dry, and squeeze it through his fingers, saying, 'Nice colour, nice colour', or 'Needs more fibre, needs more fibre', or hold it up to his nose and say, 'There is no fight in this, no fight at all', after giving it a good whiff.

CHAPTER 10

FOR THE COST OF A WATCH

Chook . . .
The sort of person to bring up nipple piercing
In front of nuns

I was pretty much prepared to piss off from Madura when the next opportunity raised its scabby head. A friend arranged for a passport, and strange as it may sound, the Bible that I tried to escape with from Krobokan was returned to me with the $1,300 still in its covers, but the passport and international driver's licence were totally useless because of water damage.

There was a guard on Madura named Doma, who we nicknamed the Donkey. He would bring anything into the prison for a price because he was always broke. Old Doma was earning $40 a month and he was married to a woman who was always pregnant. He didn't own a house or a home. Each month he had to pay rent, feed himself, his family, pay for the electricity, pay for his membership in President Soeharto's Golkar

Party and once he had paid his debts, he had to bum cigarettes off the prisoners.

One day as he was chugging down some food in my cell and filling his face with my leftovers, he picked up an English magazine that was opened up to a page that sold Rolex watches.

'Gee, for the cost of one of those watches I could be set up for life. I wouldn't have to be a prison guard any more. Funny hey, for the cost of a watch, my whole life could change,' he said.

'How much would you need to change your life, Doma?' I asked.

'A lot,' he replied, 'a lot.'

'And how much is a lot?' I asked.

'The cost of one of these watches,' he said, pointing at the open magazine's advertisement. 'With money like that I could set myself up. I could buy a house, set up a shop and still have enough to buy a good pushbike,' Doma continued.

I looked at the Rolex watch advertisement: $3,000 for a Date Just. It made me think.

Shit, the Donkey was one of the guards who spent their nights in the watchtowers – this might be my golden opportunity. So I decided to open up.

'Hey, Doma, if a bloke were to give you five-million rupees, would you help him escape from prison?' I said.

I knew that I was offering him more money than he could earn in five years as a prison guard.

'For five-million rupees, Russell, I'd throw you over the wall personally, and if they caught me, the maximum that I could get is two years in prison. If I knew one-hundred per cent that I would get five-million rupees out of it, I'd happily do the two years. You wouldn't have to pay me all the money at once, Russell, because I know it's a lot of money, and there are not a lot of people in the world with that much money. But you're a foreigner, and I trust you, that's because I think I know you. Well . . . at least enough to know that you want to try to escape again and for five-million rupees I would help you,' Doma said.

'Thanks, Doma, let me think about it for a while. Maybe we can work something out,' I said.

When Doma finally left my cell, my mind was racing.

All I needed was five-million Indonesian rupees, or less than US$3,000, to buy my way over the wall.

I called the Chook in and we talked about it. If I did piss off, there was no reason that the Chook couldn't come too. We had managed to score an extra passport that I had doctored up for him. All we needed was the money. I was sitting on $A1,300 which, at the time, was a little under $US1,000. We both decided to do our best to try to scrape up the other $US2,000.

The Chook managed $US200, and I managed just on $US1,000, so all together we had just on $US2,200.

Out of that we knew we had to arrange transport to get us both off Madura Island and over to Surabaya. This would mean we'd have to pay much, much more than the average tourist who was heading to Surabaya. Once Doma had thrown us over the walls, we would have to travel overland to Surabaya, or swim. Then, once we made it to Surabaya, we would have to fly out of the country as fast as we could, and tickets cost money.

Should we try to sail out of the country our chances would quickly dwindle. As soon as it was known that two foreigners had escaped, the whole country would be looking for us. To pull it off we needed money, or time.

Money we didn't have, but time – now, that was possible.

If Doma were to throw us over the wall at night, and the Plague could cover us for one day, I thought we could pull this plot off. After all, Barry was the Pumurka, or boss of the block. It was Barry who opened the cells in the morning and locked them up in the afternoon. No one would know if we were in or out of our cells but him, as the system of checking on the prisoners was very different on Madura than it had been in Krobokan Prison. On Madura the guards didn't do head counts, the trusted prisoners did, and Barry was our block's trusted prisoner.

A better plan could never be devised, I thought. We could be gone a bloody week before Barry reported we weren't in our cells, and no one would question him.

When we discussed this plot with Doma, he loved it.

'That's great. If you can get Barry to cover you the morning that you've gone, and he reports that you're not there in the afternoon when he has to lock you up, no one will know if you escaped on the night shift or the afternoon shift, and it would make it much safer for me,' he said.

That's when we called in the Plague to tell him about our plans and by Christ, didn't the man flip out.

If God himself had just been told that his youngest daughter wanted to study prostitution with the Devil, there's no way that God would have been as pissed off about it all as was Barry. The bastard really thought he was a guard, all those years of being the boss of the block had really warped the prick.

'Look, lads, I'm in a position of trust here and I've been given a job of trust, and that is to make my head counts every morning of the prisoners in my block and again in the afternoon. Look, I've still got two years of my sentence to serve and I don't want to get into trouble. I tried to escape once, remember, but escaping isn't the answer. Just do your time, stay out of trouble and you'll get your remission each year. Look, I've got a nine-year sentence, but I'll only have to serve seven years, that's because I got all my remission. So I'll forget about this conversation, though Doma you should be ashamed of yourself – you're a guard, you should know better,' Barry said, then off he went.

The Chook just stared dumbfounded with his jaw hanging open.

'I am sorry, I should have known Barry better. I sure hope he doesn't report me,' Doma said, as he stood up off the cell floor and left.

'I don't fucking believe it, he has just fucked up a perfect plot, and in the process told you to do your 20 years and me to do 17 years. Christ, I just can't believe it. How bent can a bloke get?' the Chook said finally, after ages of silence.

Then he too got up off the floor and left my cell, pausing at the door to look at me, with the saddest eyes God ever made.

'We could have pulled this one off, mate, we both nearly got home. How fucking bent can a bloke get?' the Chook said as he left.

I just shook my head as the Chook left. As bent as Barry, I thought to myself, as bent as Barry, that's how bent and twisted a man can get, and after that, he's no longer a man.

My next victim, of course, was Barry the Plague, and I set off after him with a passion, but the bastard was so thick-skinned it would take a bloody cruise missile to penetrate his head. The things I did to that bloke still bring goose pimples to my flesh and often make me nearly chuck.

The Chook and I fed him turd omelettes, human turds of course, but all he would do was ask for more chilli pepper or lombok and finish eating the omelette, wiping the plate clean with a piece of crust or rice.

There was one time though when I got him. We were both over at one of the prison wells one morning having a bath. As Barry was pulling up a bucket of water, I was sitting back on some big stones peeling the skin from my balls.

I had developed a fungus that makes your crotch go as red as a government post office box that has just been painted, and so itchy that you scratch it in your sleep, ripping off layers of skin. I was using some antifungal cream called Canesten, which is supposed to dry it up. But what it really does is burn like all shit and make the skin on your testicles peel off like a snake or a lizard's skin does.

I had an old toothbrush that I used to clean my toes and feet with, specialising in scraping and scratching the toenail jam out, because we all had the fungus pretty thick there too. Some of the prisoners had even lost their toenails because of it. I used this toothbrush not only to clean, but to push and force the antifungal cream under my toenails, where the infestation first starts. It was a red toothbrush – I remember its colour because it matched my balls.

As I sat back on the big stones after scrubbing my toes, with the sun beating down and drying me off, I glanced down at the old town halls. There were bits and pieces of skin sticking up everywhere. It really looked like a badly sunburnt ball bag, to say the least.

I was holding the old shaggy toothbrush in my hand, so I started to use it to pick off all the loose skin that hung off my balls like tiny curtains, brushing it through my pubic hairs that were holding other bits and pieces of skin that were stuck to my lollies. When the toothbrush bristles were full with my crusty dried knacker skin, I looked up and, low and behold, there was the Plague's toothbrush perched right next to me. It was a red one too.

The Plague had already put toothpaste on it and he had his back to me, pulling more water from the well. I picked up the toothpaste, squeezed a dash on my own skin-encrusted brush, that had a good dozen pubic hairs sticking out from it at a dozen different angles, and swapped it for Barry's.

When Barry turned around, I had already cleaned the toothpaste off his brush and was bending my head down to study my testes and pick off the bits and pieces of odd skin that I had previously overlooked, using his toothbrush.

'Leave the bastards alone or they'll fall off,' Barry said.

'But they're so itchy, mate, and look at all the skin that's coming off them. Shit, I sure hope I don't have a case of the 'No Toes'. Can you get it on the cods?' I asked.

'Gee, I don't know,' he said, as he looked down at my day-glow red balls. 'They sure do look wicked and not too many ladies would want to sleep with a bloke wearing them. They look like they would fall off on the first shake.'

He was still talking when he reached over and picked up my toothbrush, then started to clean his teeth with it.

Gotcha, I thought, and gotcha good.

But if you're going to get someone, it's really quite pointless unless they know that you've got them (except in Bartak's case – but that was different).

'Hey, Barry,' I said, as I held up his toothbrush, 'this ain't my toothbrush, it's too new. Mine was a shaggy dog.'

He instantly stopped brushing his teeth, but the brush was still in his mouth, with foam all over his lips and dribbling down his jaw, his eyes growing wider and wider.

'Hey, let me have a look at that brush,' I said.

He pulled it out of his mouth as slowly as if it were a bomb he was holding on the verge of exploding, and carefully holding it out a good distance from his face, he started to study it quite minutely, and with great interest.

I moved up beside him and said, 'Look, see, there, that's one of my pubes,' pointing at what looked like the legs of a mashed-up spider sticking out the sides of the toothbrush. 'That's my ball brush, you bent bastard, give it back. Shit, I don't know where your mouth has been, and you're using my personal cod-scrubber to wash your filthy teeth. Christ, mate, friendship can only go so far you know.' I snatched it out of his hand.

I bent down and washed my old toothbrush in the bucket of water that Barry had just pulled up from the well, emptying it out in the process.

That's when Barry fully clicked on and started wiping his mouth and spitting foam all over the place faster than a score of rabid dogs, ripping the bucket out of my hands and throwing it down the well to get some water to wash out his mouth with.

'You twisted cocksucker,' he spat, 'you swapped brushes.'

'Now mate, settle down,' I said. 'Shit, look, you forgot to hold onto the rope, now how are we going to get the bucket back up?'

Barry quickly glanced down into the well, realising his mistake. Once you dropped the bucket down into the well, you had to hang onto the other end of the rope so you could pull the bucket up again.

'Motherfucker,' he spat and bolted off naked to one of the other wells in another block desperately looking for water.

The Chook had just turned up at the well for a bath as Barry the Plague dashed past him with white foam smeared all over his face and down his arms, which he had used in a desperate bid to try and rub his own lips off his face.

'Got him, uh?' the Chook asked, with a grin on his face. 'How?'

'With this,' I said, holding up my red toothbrush, smiling.

'Ooh, nasty, nasty,' the Chook said, shaking his half-bald brown head with a grim smile. His toothbrush was green.

During my time in Madura Island's punishment prison, I gained a reputation. Half the prisoners and guards thought I was a little mad, the other half were totally sure that I was.

I spent the whole time in that prison either planning a new escape or choosing a new victim to inflict my frustrations on.

I didn't smoke cigarettes, but everywhere I went prisoners or guards would ask me for one. I decided to buy them and offer them around freely to keep everyone happy.

There was a small group of local prisoners who I had become close to. In the afternoons we would all get together and play Chess, Seven Scop or Yahtzee, and that's when the guards would get all friendly so as to bludge whatever they could from us.

In the afternoon the prison workshops would be closed, and so too was the prison visiting room. Whenever the prisoners got a visit, the guards would rip-off more than half of the goodies that the prisoners were given by their family or friends.

This part of the prison system used to really piss me off. To watch a prisoner be given a carton of ciggies, a kilo of sugar and coffee, and a pack of biscuits from his family, and then watch as the prison guards took half of it off him, really cut against my grain.

One day, while one of the more greedy guards was on his shift, he dropped into my block bludging ciggies from the local prisoners who had just had visits, and who had already been taxed their 50 per cent by the other guards.

The guard's name was Kami, but I called him Cunti.

'I'd bet my brother's left ball that Kami comes over here to score some ciggies,' said one of the prisoners who was a Surabayan hit man.

'I'll bet my sister's chastity,' replied another who had run over two policemen, accidentally killing the rider of the motorcycle straight off. The second policeman, who was the pillion passenger, he had to chase for nearly a kilometre before he could accidentally run him over too.

'I hope he does,' I said, as I pulled out a cigarette from one of the two packs that were lying open on the floor of the cell where we were playing.

Londo, the killer cat, was sprawled out alongside me deep in sleep, lying down with his big pink balls and crusty black arse facing me. I tickled his balls with the filter of the cigarette and the dirty bastard started to purr.

'He likes that,' the cop killer said.

'Better than your sister's chastity,' the Hit Man said.

Then I jabbed the filter of the cigarette up Londo's arse.

'Meow, meow . . . wow,' Londo screamed and ran off.

The prisoners just looked at me in wonder as I replaced the cigarette, leaving it half poking out from the packet. Giving them a smile, I called out to Kami.

'Hey, Pak, Pak, I need a witness, have a look at these dice,' I said, as I got Kami's attention and he came over to my cell.

'I need a four to win, double ones, or three and one. Wish me luck,' I said, and threw double sixes.

'Good numbers,' he replied.

'Too high, I lose,' I said, as I picked up the packet of ciggies.

'Like a cigarette, Pak?' I asked, as I offered him the cancer stick that I had just rammed up the cat's arse.

'Yeah, don't mind if I do,' he replied, taking the offered dotch, lighting it up, picking some small black lumps off the filter, and headed off searching for other tasties he could bludge off the other prisoners.

When he had gone, Cop Killer and Hit Man broke up. My friendship with them was solidified. I had gained the respect of two very bad, good men and it seemed they liked my style.

I did everything I could do to break the monotony of prison life, from pissing into the air cooler in the prison director's office, to setting off a hepatitis scare throughout the prison.

Actually, I managed to infect 25 per cent of the prisoners with the shit, piss and spit of Akmed who was dying of hepatitis. I was so successful in that caper that I ended up on the floor myself, as yellow as the guts of a mango for two whole months.

Once I was back on my feet it didn't take me long to find something else to keep me busy. I discovered a couple of rotten bricks in the wall beside the ladies' block of the prison, so I started to pick them out.

There were only nine women in the block and they all looked beautiful, even the 63-year-old grandmother who ate one of her grandchildren. But Christ, who was I to get involved in family squabbles?

Those picked-out bricks were kept a secret for nearly a month, but all good things have to come to an end.

I was caught red-handed – well my hands weren't really red, but I was caught standing on two bricks with my pants down and part of me sticking into the women's block.

Monic, who was one of the lady prisoners I had grown to know – so to speak – was doing her best to pull me through into the women's block by the stork when I was sprung. Another week was all I needed, and I am sure I could have got my head through that hole, or Monic sure would have got her head through.

I was marched up to the KPLP office to see the security chief, my boss in the cock-breeding racket, Mr Bartak. After all, there had been a hole made in one of the prison walls, security had been breached, so security had to rectify the problem.

Now that I am writing this all down, I really must admit that old Mr Bartak was a pretty decent bloke when it's all boiled down.

The little bugger had the power of life and death in that prison. He could have had anything done to me, anything from sending me to the punishment blocks to sending me out to work in the salt fields.

The salt fields are where the ocean comes in at night at high tide and deposits salt water. When the tide goes back out, the seawater is caught on this big open flat area of the beach that stretches for miles.

As the sun evaporates the water, the salt from the sea is left behind. To scrape the salt up, you have to do it when it's at its hardest and driest, and that's at midday when the temperature is well over 100° Fahrenheit, when the heat and whiteness of the salt and the sand are intensified by the blazing glowing sun. The prisoners who worked in the salt fields were the most regular visitors to the prison's two morgues.

It was one of the last places to seek employment, but as it turned out Mr Bartak had other plans for me. He didn't want to loose his star cock breeder and trainer on the salt fields. Maybe I've neglected to mention how successful the last couple of cocks had been.

Mujiano and I worked pretty well together, and we worked and exercised the cocks well also. We had all day and every day to train, groom and build them up into top fighting condition and we both had our experience to fall back on.

Pak Mujiano had the experience of over 35 years of working with fighting cocks. I had my own useful experience: I knew about performance-enhancing drugs. There are drugs you can stick into the largest or slowest creature that will turn it into an Olympian: Ritalin, Tenuate, Pemoline, Ronyl, Volital, or a dozen or so other stimulants. All of which can get anything from a horse to a chicken in its top fighting or running condition.

Since I had been working with Pak Mujiano our cocks had become 80 per cent winners. So that's more than likely why Bartak decided not to send me on a punishment detail after trying to break into the women's block. It was better for him to keep me working with the cocks and filling his pockets at the cockfights. So instead of the salt fields he sent me to a whorehouse (God bless you, Mr Bartak, may you live 1,000 years).

After three years without a woman, apart from Monic and that all happened within the space of a brick, I was shattered. When I got my first real lady I became a dissolving jelly (and you can take that literally).

Every time I tried to stick it in between those sweet open thighs, I blew my bolt.

'Relax, relax,' the hooker said. I wouldn't remember her today if I fell over her, because from the moment I entered the room of the whorehouse I couldn't tear my eyes away from her tasty brown legs and her little fluffy patch of paradise.

It's all very hard to explain and it would embarrass not only me, but you too, so I won't tell you how I ended up with sperm in my ears and hair, or how I kept on climaxing with a softie, or how I ended up with the traces of freshly painted nail and toe polish in my mouth, not to mention more hair in my mouth than Max Jackson has got on his head, leaving the poor girl looking like a plucked duck from below the navel. All I can say is that when I hit that hooker, the first lady that I had open access to for three years, I acted like an atomic-powered dildo on supercharge.

After the first frustrating hour, which turned out to be about three and a half minutes, I was a trembling mess and still I hadn't had sex with her, at least not in the way the Pope would imagine it.

'Wow,' she said. 'You foreigners are wild.'

We spent the next forever just sitting on the bed talking. When I told her I was a prisoner from the big prison up the road and that I hadn't had a woman for three years, I started to cry. As I sobbed away she cuddled me and started to cry also.

'Oh, you poor man, I didn't know, they didn't tell me, oh how cruel they are, I could never go that long without . . . oh, how you must have suffered without this,' she said, as she held my hand over her breast, and I could feel the bouncing and flickering of her nipple through my fingers.

'Yes, yes, you're so right, I've been treated so cruel, so cruel,' I whimpered, as I crawled between her legs.

We spent the next eternity crying until I was on the verge of my first climax inside a woman. Just as I was about to let go and burst my three years of loneliness, pain, suffering and frustration into this thrusting gulf of God, this pulsating piece of paradise, flapping flaps of fantasy, the bitch stopped her tears and thrusting pelvis, and in the straightest of voices, totally devoid of all emotion said, '5,000 rupees extra, or I'll pop you out – your time's up.'

'You're joking,' I said.

But she wasn't, she popped me out on the last thrust and I lost it on the sheets. When I was taken back to the prison that day, I was feeling probably the worst that I have ever felt in my life, and for the sake of a filthy 5,000 rupee or $US3.00, I could have returned feeling like a million dollars. She wouldn't give me credit. Whoever said hookers have got hard hearts are 100 per cent correct, they truly can have hard, money-hungry hearts. But being the prince of men that I am, I still love them all.

CHAPTER 11

SHAKE ME, WAKE ME WHEN IT'S OVER

Many of nature's most noble creatures
Are of a fugitive kind

As things turned out, Bartak rewarded me once or twice a month with a visit to the local complex or brothel. So as long as the cocks were winning, I started to gain access to the outside world and that's when I really discovered just how hard it would be to get off the island without help. But as the time passed, I was allowed out more often from the prison whenever there was an important cockfight, with only one guard to accompany me.

As the months passed all I had to do was pack up a cock in its basket, tell Bartak where the important fight was, and he would send a guard with me to carry the cock. I ended up having the run of the place. Whenever I got the urge, I'd jump into a *becak* or *trishaw*, which in Indonesia and throughout Asia was a common mode of transport built to carry passengers, and head off to get my rocks off.

HELL'S PRISONER

I started to become native in my lifestyle. The thoughts of running away began to fade. The more and more fights the cocks won, the less and less I would have to be in the prison. The people in the town of Parmakasan started to get to know me and I was learning to speak the language quite well.

Whenever I passed a cockfight house or pit, the owners would call out, 'Saul, Saul,' which is the end sound of the name Russell, or Russ-Saul in Indonesian. Indonesians use the end of your name, whereas in the West they use the first part. In the West a bloke named Russell is given Russ as his nickname, in Indonesia the nickname of Russell becomes Sell, pronounced Saul.

'Hey, Saul, there's a fight tonight,' or 'Saul, bring back that pack of feathers next Sunday.' There was always someone who would yell out something like, 'Saul, when Fire fights again let me know.'

'And why should I do that, so you can make a handsome profit? What profit is there in that for me?' I'd say.

'The promise of a second Fire fight for free' would be the expected reply from the local happy houses.

During these days Akbar II was still too young to fight, but Mujiano and I had trained a new champion – his name was Fire because of his colour and hot moods. He was one bad-arsed cock. In 30 fights, he had won every one with quick clean kills and he was not even two years old, which is still young for a fighting cock.

Fire quickly gained a reputation, so whenever there was a big-money fight I was allowed out of the prison to handle him. That's because fighting cocks, like all animals, respond better with their handlers or someone they know and trust around them than they would with a stranger.

Every time that I took Fire out of the prison for a fight, in some weird way it felt as though I too were going out to battle. When one of the big nights came and some cocks from Java were brought over to Madura Island to clean up the Village Kings, as the Maduranese cocks were referred to by the Javanese, the betting was much heavier than usual.

As I squatted down to watch the fights, caressing the feathers of Fire through his cage, Mrs Watty, who was one of the prison guards who worked in the office, squatted down beside me. Mrs Watty was a good-looking woman by any man's standards with a top little trim body that was quite obvious to the blindest of blokes, even in her daggy green prison uniform.

But on this night she was wearing tight jeans and a T-shirt with the sleeves cut off. As she reached over to pat Fire, I could see down the cut sleeves of her T-shirt that her boobs were nice and she wasn't wearing a bra.

'Will he win tonight?' she asked.

'Has he ever lost?' I replied, with a grin forged with confidence.

She looked up at me, flicking back her wild mop of black hair and our eyes met. We just stared at each other for what seemed a very long time. It was as though we were both seeing something for the first time but knew it well. She broke the moment by saying, 'You're a very handsome man, Saul, I'll follow your advice, and when Fire fights, I'll put 10,000 rupee on him. Don't let him fight until I come back. I'm going to get a drink. Would you like a beer?'

Before I could answer she was off, pushing her way though the crowd. My eyes were glued to her butt and the way her tight jeans looked like they were painted on it, and how sensuously swinging her hips were. Now that's one hell of a tasty woman, I thought. When Bartak squatted beside me, I was still watching Watty's top little body push its way through the crowd to score some drinks.

'She's not a woman to take as a second or even third wife. Just look at her, her husband has been dead only two years, and already she's looking for a new one. She's already old, and she still thinks she's new,' Bartak said, as he started to chuckle.

'I didn't know that she was a widow,' I said.

'Oh, yeah, her husband died over two years ago and in Indonesia no good Islamic man would take a woman like her now. Look how old she is,' he said.

'How old is she?' I asked

'Twenty-seven,' he replied, 'And in five years of marriage she couldn't produce a single child for her husband. The poor man, may Allah watch over him, was left with no children.' Bartak was on the verge of expanding his thoughts on Mrs Watty, when he noticed her pushing her way back through the crowd towards us.

When she squatted down beside us, she handed me a beer and offered him another. He politely refused, got up and went his own way. Then she started to drink out of the can that she had offered him, laughing, saying, 'I am glad he didn't take it, otherwise I would have had to battle all those bags of sweat to go and buy another.' She clunked my can and said, 'What's the English word?'

'Ahh, cheers, cheers to a good night and a fiery win,' I replied, tapping her can with mine.

We spent the next hour talking, and I discovered a lot about the little lady. As Indonesians go, she was a very modern and Western-orientated lady. By Indonesian standards, as a widow of 27, she may have been classified as an old lady but by Western standards, she was still a young woman with the world at her feet.

When Fire had his fight he was true to form. As quick and deadly as ever, he killed his first opponent within seconds, much less than a full minute. Only if you have watched or witnessed cockfights could you really appreciate that time.

Watty came squealing back to me with her hands full of rupees, trying to stick half in my pocket. She said, 'You take half, you earned it.'

'No, you made the bet, it's your winnings,' I said, as I pulled the money back out of my pocket and returned it to her. At first she refused to take it, so I grabbed her by the hand and pulled her towards me. I looked for a pocket that I could stick it back in but she was only wearing a sleeveless T-shirt. She started to laugh.

'I have no pockets,' she said, thrusting out her small chest. 'You have to take the money.'

Well, there were other pockets and places that I could have stuck it – her jeans' pocket for instance – but it would have only gained us both bad reputations.

'Well, can I at least buy the next beer?' I asked.

My God, this is a cheeky woman, I thought, why haven't I noticed her before? I see her every day in the prison offices when I go to torment someone so why haven't I noticed her? Christ, she thinks I'm handsome! So off we went to the local *wawung*, or night stall, me holding onto Fire in his cage and Watty holding onto my hand. We spent the next few hours discovering each other more.

When Bartak turned up at the now closing wawung, he was pretty drunk, but very happy, with a prison guard who was just as drunk and who was supposed to be watching over me, behind him.

'Hey Saul,' Bartak said, 'What do you think about putting Fire out to stud for a month? My friend here will look after him?' He pointed to another local bloke holding an empty cage in his hand who was standing beside him, and he didn't look happy.

'Actually he's my brother and he always bets against my cocks, but now he wants to breed with one. What do you think Saul? Should we trust him for a month with Fire?'

'Well, if he's your brother, Pak, who else can you trust? Besides, Fire could do with a rest, not to mention a little bit of *pokkie*,' I said, which caused everyone to laugh. Pokkie in Indonesian means fanny, or nookie in English. When the laughter died down, Bartak threw one arm over his brother's shoulder and ordered the half-charged guard to pick up Fire's cage and follow him.

When he had gone four or five metres, he stopped in his tracks and returned to where Watty and I were standing in the cockfighting area of the closing night markets. 'You're a guard of the prison, Mrs Watty, and this man is a prisoner of Madura. I officially hand him over to you to return him to the prison,' he said, as he smiled, then continued, 'sometime tomorrow.' He went, leaving Watty and me alone in the night market.

'So, I am your prisoner. Where do we go now?' I said.

'Do you like to dance? There's a disco on Madura and no one would ever know who you were – you're far too handsome to look like a daggy prisoner,' she said.

'Take me to your disco, madam,' I said, holding up my arms, 'I am a victim of love.'

'You're crazy,' she said, as she grabbed onto my hands, pulling them down, and off we went to dance the night away. When the disco closed and we had both taken well over our average doses of fortified beverages, we walked the quiet village streets of Madura with the occasional distant yapping of street dogs, Watty with one arm around my waist and mine draped over her shoulder.

'Where are we going?' I asked. 'We can't go back to the prison like this, someone might ask questions.'

'The prison isn't open, silly, my place is just up on the corner,' she giggled.

When we arrived at her apartment, she placed one of her soft thin index fingers over my lips, and the other, she held up to her own lips and started to smile. I stuck my tongue out and started to lick her finger and she began to giggle even more. She started to push her small open hand into my face and I opened my mouth, swallowing half her hand. She started to laugh even more, pulling her fingers out from my mouth. I pulled her towards me and covered her lips with mine; it was the sweetest kiss that I had had for years.

When I first entered Watty's little apartment, the memories of a lifetime long passed rushed through my mind. It was the apartment of a woman. An apartment of a woman not rich, not poor, but of a woman with her own tastes. Her place was beautiful and far too delicate for a man to be living in.

'So what do you think?' she said, with a wave of her arm. 'This is home.'

'And where is the bed?' I asked.

'You're my captive, handsome, I'll tell you that when I like and I'll ask the questions; it's behind that screen,' she said, as she held up her small, thin, delicately shaped arm, pointing to one side of the room with a beautifully tapered finger.

'Ahh, so that's where we go,' I said, picking her up off her feet and carrying her behind the silk painted screen.

Our lovemaking that night was just that: lovemaking. Watty had not slept with another man since the death of her husband, and he had been the only man that she had ever had. Even though she had worn the tight Western jeans and cut off T-shirts and loved to dance, now at the age of 27 she had very little likelihood of ever finding a new husband, all because of the Indonesian traditions and culture. That night I made up for three years and Watty made up for a lifetime.

When I returned to the prison the following day, I was walking on clouds. My life on Madura had changed. I stopped searching for people I could inflict my hatred or frustrations on and took every opportunity that I could find to get out of the prison to see Watty.

Whenever I saw her in the prison office, we would stop to pass a few words with each other, but never for too long. A lot of people were already aware of our relationship, or were very suspicious of it, and we didn't want to flaunt it. A majority of the guards, both male and female, felt sorry for Watty and genuinely liked her. In their eyes she was a widow, who was doomed to spend the rest of her life childless and without a husband, alone, but fate had other plans for Watty, as it did for me, as it does for all of us.

My visits to Watty's little apartment opened my eyes to how civilised people should live, the way life should be – not the way it was for the prisoners on Madura.

I went on a crusade to improve the conditions of the other prisoners. Don't ask me why I did this, maybe it was because life for me at that time was so full that I felt that I wanted to share my happiness with the others to get them all better food, or medicine when they needed it, clothes for their backs and pants to cover their bare arses, soap to wash with, and lights in their cells, whether it be from bulbs or candles.

The day that I really made up my mind was the day two rats were killed in the prison kitchen. The two big fat buggers were caught in one of the storerooms where the rice was kept. Only the prison guard, who was the head guard of the kitchen, was allowed to go in there, along with the prisoner who was the kitchen boss.

The prison guard's name was Darmorrow and once a week he would call up the kitchen boss, along with two trustees and pull out a few bags of rice, enough to feed the prisoners for a week, then move it to one of the storerooms beside the big cookers.

When Darmorrow discovered the rats in the main storeroom, he got pissed off. But he couldn't blame the prisoners because the rats had come in via his office, which sided the main storeroom. They had chewed their way through the walls of his office into the storeroom. He had no choice but to pull out all the bags of rice and check for more rats and more holes, then repair those that he found.

When all the rice was pulled out from the main storeroom I was amazed at how much there was and how little was used of it each week to feed the prisoners – barely any. There was something very wrong with this set up. All of that rice and so many empty stomachs. Something had to be done, I thought, but what?

As I wandered around the prison deep in thought, I passed Block E, which was at the back of the punishment cells and connected up with the prison infirmary. I noticed two prisoners cooking at an open fire. They seemed really happy, giggling and chuckling away with each other, as one of them waved a piece of cardboard under the fire to make it hotter. I started to pull out of my thoughts as I watched them and I smiled.

The Chook walked over and said, 'Looks like the boys have got a cook-up going, let's go and check it out.' As we headed over towards them to check out what they were cooking, the Chook continued, 'Looks like two fried turds.'

'Smells like it too,' I replied.

'What you got here?' the Chook asked one of the prisoners fanning the fire.

'Want some?' the prisoner said.

'Oh yeah, I might have a go at it, what is it?' the Chook asked again.

'We got them from the kitchen, they were caught stealing the rice, one of the kitchen prisoners gave them to us, along with some chillies and ginger. Wait here, I've got some rice too,' he said, and off he went to some nearby bushes. Pulling out a black plastic bag, he gave a fleeting look around the compound as though he were expecting bandits to pounce on him at any minute. He then returned to where we were, opened his plastic bag of rice and evenly distributed a couple of handfuls of gungy grey rice onto four sections of a banana leaf.

I was watching what was being cooked up in fascination because I still wasn't 100 per cent sure what they were, but when what looked to me like small bones started to stick out of the two turds that were being fried up, it hit me, '*Tikus*,' I said.

'Two big ones, still fresh, only caught this morning,' the bloke fanning the fire said, as he nodded and smiled.

'That's not tikus, as in fucking tikus is it?' the Chook asked.

'Yep, that's what it is. Meet the two rats that got into the rice room this morning, Rastus and Raffles, the two wee rodents . . . now deceased,' I said.

'You must be going soft, six months ago you would have told me only after I had tasted the bastards. How did you know they were rats? I mean, they've got no tails, legs or heads, how did you pick 'em?' the Chook said, looking at me.

'Only when the little bones started to stick through the meat. I was in the kitchen this morning when they were caught. Christ, I don't believe it, how hungry must these poor bastards have to be to happily fry up a couple of rats to eat. It's wrong, it's totally wrong,' I said.

'Yeah, well I suppose it is but then again so is this whole place. It's life, mate, and at least these rats were caught in the kitchen, where they were getting good tucker. Christ, imagine eating one of those bastards that live in the shitters, now that would be wrong,' he said, starting to smile.

So we wandered off, politely refusing to partake in the meal and talked about the different things that we had seen the other prisoners eat. The list was endless, ranging from beetles and bugs of all sorts, to crickets, grasshoppers and praying mantis. Spiders were used as a traditional medicine, so too were cobwebs, and lizards of all shapes, sizes and colours. Any and all birds that were game enough to fly over the prison, or even sillier enough to land and nest in one of the prison blocks, found their way into the cooking pot. Eggshells were eaten or crushed up with various herbs and used as remedies for everything from skin rashes and dysentery to dizzy spells, fading vision, baldness and any type of black magic you could name – eggshells always seemed to be part of the mixture.

That's why old Pak Mujiano in Block F so jealously guarded all empty chicken shells – and sold them only when the price was right. Whenever a chicken died in its cage, Mujiano would chop it up and swap the bits and pieces for extra rice (not prison rice, but uncooked rice from the outside that the other prisoners' families had sent in), or for things that his mates, the other PKI prisoners in his block, needed.

Mujiano didn't want for much because Bartak looked after him, and so did I. But he had seven other ageing PKI prisoners in his block, who had come to rely on him over the more than 20 years they had been together for their food, soap, clothes, the occasional cup of coffee or tea with sugar and, most importantly, medicine.

Mujiano was in his mid-fifties, the rest of his PKI mates were in their sixties and seventies, so I guess you could say he looked after them like a son would.

The prisoners in Block F lived better than the rest of the convicts on Madura, but that was only because Mujiano was such a good breeder and trainer of cockfighters and because his heart was big, he cared for his friends. He was much like old Pak Puji in Krobokan, and we got on well together. Mujiano was fluent in English, German, Javanese, Maduranese, Russian, Indonesian and one or two other Indonesia languages .

Mujiano had gone to university in East Germany and on his return he had joined the PKI, Indonesia's Communist Party and quickly moved up in its ranks. We often talked about communism, capitalism and international politics, or about religion, the arts, music, the present-day fashions and history. Our talks and debates were always quite stimulating. We both had small short-wave radios, so we could listen to the news of the world every night. He listened to Radio Moscow, Germany's Dutch Avella and America's VOA and I would listen to the BBC, ABC and VOA. The following morning we would discuss what we had heard the night before while we cleaned, groomed and trained the cocks.

The day after the Chook and I had seen the two prisoners cooking up the two rats, I talked to Mujiano about the prisoner's conditions.

'"The Time has come, the Walrus said, to talk of many things . . . of shoes and ships, and ceiling wax, and cabbages and kings." Have you ever heard that poem before, Mujiano?' I asked.

'Please repeat it, it sounds familiar,' he said, as he stopped what he was doing.

So I did. When I had finished, he was smiling as he looked down at a small chick he was tenderly holding.

'Yes, I've heard that poem before, a lifetime ago, when I was a small boy in England. My parents were there for a time and I had a nanny, an English nanny, it's only now that you have reminded me of it. Don't tell me that they still teach those same silly poems in Australia,' Mujiano said.

'It's not so silly, Mujiano, it's just something that I've been thinking, that's all,' I said, as I started to clean out one of the cages.

'And what are you thinking, Saul?' he asked.

'That the time has come,' I said, dropping the cleaning brush on the floor of the cage. 'Look at this,' I said, as I stuck my hand into one of my pockets, dropping rice into his hand. 'Then look at this,' I said, as I pulled out another handful of rice from another pocket and dropped it into his other hand. 'Look at it, see the difference, that is what the time is all about. In one hand you hold the rice of a free man, the rice that the people outside these walls eat. See how white and clean it is, and in the other hand you hold the prison rice, look at it, it's full of husks and weevils' shit, dirt and stones. We both know that the guards are swapping the government rice that is sent to the prison for this shit rice that they feed the prisoners, and they're not even generous with their shit. Sure, you and I fill our bellies well, but the corruption in this place makes me sick. I've watched dozens of prisoners die because they weren't given food or medicine. How many hundreds have you seen die for the same reason? Surely you must know that Darmorrow is selling the prison food outside and he could never pull it off without the director or Bartak being in the know.'

'Look, look,' I said, as I pulled out a copy of the United Nations Vienna Convention on the treatment of prisoners (which Indonesia had recently signed) that I had smuggled into the prison. 'Look at this, read it, then tell me what you think the prisoners here would do if they could read this?' I said.

Mujiano dropped the two handfuls of rice on the ground, took the papers that I had offered him and started to read. He went quiet.

'Where did you get this, Saul?' Mujiano asked ten minutes later.

'From my friend who works for Amnesty International,' I replied.

'And what do you intend to do with this? Have you shown it to any of the guards or other prisoners?' he asked.

'What would be the reason? The ones who can speak English, or even read it, I could count on my fingers,' I said.

'Well, in a way, that's good, because what you have here could cause a lot of problems if it were to be passed around, even in its English writing – it could upset a lot of things. At the moment you have the ability to leave the prison with the cocks when they fight. If you were to lose that, there are other things you would lose too. Would you risk all that?' he said, and we both knew what the other things were and they weren't just the cockfights.

'I'll leave this copy with you, Mujiano. Read it all and we'll talk about it tomorrow, or the day after, but for now put it in a safe place,' I said, as I got up and went over to Akbar II's cage.

I spent the rest of the day massaging Akbar's legs, chest, wings, neck and tail, even flipping him. All this was necessary to exercise the bird. When flipping a fighting cock, you hold his wings down into his body then flip him upside down. A good cock will always land on his feet and the same goes when you twist him. Hold his wings back and twist him quickly in the air, as you throw him up, left or right. Just like a cat, he will always land on his feet, but it's how he lands that will tell you if he is a good fighter. If he lands with two feet flat on the deck, he'd be dead within seconds in a cockfight, where his opponent would be wearing three-inch razor-sharp blades attached to his spurs. A good fighting cock doesn't try to land on the ground with his feet or claws, he comes down with his spurs, trying to slash his enemy with them and when he's got three to, sometimes, five inches of razor-sharp steel tied to his spurs, he does damage.

The next day Mujiano handed me back the papers I had given him.

'The plans of a perfect society, how easy they are to write on paper, but to put them into reality, that's where the difficulty lies. We both know that the system in my country, as it is, is destroyed by the seeds of corruption. We all want something better, whether it be a totally new society, or just a better car than our neighbour. Corruption has many colours, Saul, pure black and pure white become corrupted by grey. Orange, green and blue are corrupted by brown and that's the colour of the earth. So, Saul, can you really look into your heart and tell me that this grey, this orange, or brown are corruptions, or something unnatural in life?' he said.

'You've twisted the truth,' I said, getting angry with him. 'Tell me, what colours are there between life and death? Because that's all I see in this prison: life and death.'

'There are many colours for truth, just as there are for justice . . . and dying. Death has many colours too, Saul. Look around you, all of us, each and every one of us, the way we live, think and breathe is coloured by life. Yes, life is coloured by living, and each has its shades of dying. Learn from them and accept what you have.'

'I understand your philosophy well, Mujiano, but it's not mine. The now is the present, but the future I have no control of, so now that I can control the present, I'll grab it by the throat. I am going to make Indonesian translations of that Vienna Convention and pass it on to all the other prisoners who can read and, if I get a chance, I'll send copies on to all the other prisoners I know held in other prisons in this country,' I said, as I stood up, holding the pamphlet in my hand.

'Spoken like a true revolutionary,' he said, smiling.

'The time has come, the Walrus said, to talk of many things, of shoes and ships and ceiling wax, and cabbages and kings,' I said.

'How will you change the world? And who will be the king?' he said.

'I don't intend to change the world, mate, but the time has come to get the prisoners together and do something about all these empty bellies,' I said.

'And what laurels will they place upon your head? Do you wish to be a king of prisoners that you are already, with the privileges that you have? Is it your wish to lead a thousand prisoners to a quicker death and more suffering then they now have? You can't change the world, Saul. The foundations of mankind were set and dried long, long before you were born. Will you waste your life like I have wasted mine, believing that the world can change for the better? Is that your destiny, one that would lead a thousand men to their graves if they follow you? You may think the time is ripe in this prison for rebellion, but what then? What will you do when you and your friends are crushed into the ground? And that's what they will do to you, they will crush you and your friends into the dirt and the only crown you will wear will be the one made of stone, which marks your grave,' Mujiano said.

'If that is to be my destiny, then so be it,' I replied.

The following week things heated up. I had translated the Vienna Convention of the Treatment of Prisoners into Indonesian. I had sent copies of it to over a score of different prisons, with the help of the Hit Man, Cop Killer and half a dozen of their mates, who also had brothers, fathers, cousins, uncles, and one, two or three grandfathers in prisons scattered throughout Indonesia.

While I was making the translations from English into Indonesian, I still had access to the outside to do all my photocopying and posting. At first I tried to hide what I was doing from Watty, but it was hard. She picked up on all the new words that I had learnt, words like *Memperbedakan*.

'Now that's a big word,' she said. 'What does it mean in English?'

'To discriminate,' I said.

'And where did you learn that new word,' she asked.

'In the dictionary, I stumbled on it the other night,' I said.

'Is that what you do at night when you're in the prison, just study the dictionary?' she asked.

'Well there's not much more that I can do, apart from listen to my radio, or sleep. What else is there to do?' I asked.

'Well, I study this photo,' she replied, 'It's of the handsomest *Londo* in the world, he's really no good, but his smile is number one, and the rest of him is number ten.'

'Oh yeah, we'll just have to see about that,' I said, as I attacked her, holding her arms back and thrusting my tongue into her ear every chance I got.

'Stop it, stop it you animal,' she cried, 'Don't you have any respect, I am your guard, Londo, and the door's not locked so get up and lock it,' she said as she bit me softly on the lower lip. 'And get those pants off – and that's an order.'

Sometimes Watty would call me Saul and sometimes she would call me Londo, which in Indonesian slang means Dutchie or Dutchman; it can also mean any foreigner. It's quite a derogatory term, depending on how it's used. But when Watty called me Londo, it was with affection – well at least most times.

Over the year we'd been together, Watty's English had become nearly as good as my own, if not better. When Australian Embassy officials phoned, she was asked to talk to them and answer their questions, which all in all were pretty straightforward. 'How are you? Are the Australian prisoners still there? Are they still alive? Nice weather we're having here in Jakarta. How's the weather where you are? Sucks, hey. Well, we'll phone again in a month or two, goodbye.' Watty answered all the important diplomatic questions she was asked, so she was promoted to prison interpreter, which delighted her extremely.

'Why does the embassy ask to talk to me?' she asked me one night when we were alone.

'Because they know you're so beautiful and you can speak such good English,' I said.

'Oh, Saul, why are you a prisoner? Why can't I keep you here with me forever? Wouldn't you like to stay with me forever? I'll bet you would,' she said, pushing me down on the floor and throwing her leg over me. As her wild black locks covered her face and shoulders, her arms pinned me to the floor with her face half covered in the shadows of her hair. A flickering candle lightened one side of her small delicate face. Her features were reminiscent of a work of fine art, designed and created by a superior craftsman.

'Oh, Saul, why is life so cruel? Why did you ever come into my life?'

Then I noticed the tear in her eye as she stared down at me. As it built up and ran its course, running down her cheek and then onto my chest, I realised that there were other tears falling, also from her cheek, that were hidden in the shadows of her wild falling locks of hair.

'What's the problem, Watty? Why are you crying, little lady?' I asked, then I thought, ah, you're a woman and women, just like men, need to cry sometimes, and when we do, we need someone to cuddle us, and tell us, yeah, it's OK, I am lonely too. The world really is a hard place if you have no one to love you and cuddle you when you're feeling miserable.

I pulled her down towards me and held her in my arms as she sobbed her heart out. 'It's OK, I'm here,' I said, as I held her close to me, 'It's OK, I am here, I am here Watty, no one can hurt you, I am here,' I said, as she snuggled her face into my neck. I could feel her tears run down my skin. As

I slowly ran one hand through her hair, clearing those wild locks from her face, her sobs died down.

'Has anyone told you you're beautiful tonight? If they have I'm jealous,' I said. This brought a smile to her face.

'No one has ever told me I am beautiful, except you,' she said.

'Ah, so you see, that shows how stupid men are. We're either blind or totally stupid, there's just so much we forget to do and say, but then again we're not like you ladies, we've got muscles in our heads,' I said as I kissed away her tears. 'We need to be told or we don't understand. We blokes are pretty thick, we don't understand why those we care about get so upset, well at least I don't. Why all these tears?' I asked.

'Because I, because I, I love you, Saul. I love you with all my heart,' she paused then very softly said, 'I must die. I knew that it would have to happen, but I wasn't expecting to meet you, Londo, I never thought that it would be this way. I don't want to die, not now, I want to live, I want to do all the things other people do. I didn't know that to love someone would hurt me so. But you, Saul, oh, Saul, I don't want to die any more, I love you,' she finished, as she broke up crying in my arms.

That's when I learnt that Watty had cancer, of the worst type – advanced and probably deadly.

When she told me of it that night, I stayed strong, as strong as a man can be who is in fear of losing his heart, but doesn't want his body to know. She told me she had to travel to Jakarta for an operation – and that the odds were not good. We made love that night with a deepness that I am too inarticulate to explain. It was soft, it was gentle and it was loving on the scale that would tear your heart and soul out.

I was full of tears that I held inside as Watty lay in my arms in the early hours of the morning. While holding each other tight, she whispered, 'Thank you, Saul, for showing me love. It's a gift I'll now die with. It's something I've not felt before, it is really beautiful.'

'Don't talk like that,' I said. 'The doctors in Jakarta can do miracles, when you get back I'll still be here and if I have to escape from the prison,

I'll be here in this little room to make you the first cup of tea.'

She giggled at this then, as she cuddled up closer to me, she said, in a whisper full of mockery and love, 'Why haven't you tried to escape before, Londo, you could have broken away from my small arms a long, long time ago. Just as you could this very minute, you could have done it so many times before, why didn't you try?'

'Because I am very comfortable here,' I said as I snuggled my face into her wild thick locks of hair and nibbled on her ear lobe.

'Tell me what's in your heart, Saul. Tell me?' she asked, as she moved away gracefully, brushing those thick locks away from my face.

When I looked at her beautiful face, as she held my hands in hers, we both broke into huge smiles.

'You love me, you creep, you really love me. That's why you didn't try to run away,' she said.

'Well, you're partly right, but you're wrong with the creep bit,' I said, and with that she bit me on the lip.

She ran her tongue over my lips, kissing the one that she had just bitten so tenderly, and said, 'Say it, or I'll bite your lip off.'

'I love you, Watty,' I said, as I reached up and grabbed her. 'And when you get back from Jakarta, this place won't be big enough.'

'Big enough for what?' she said, as our lips met again.

'Big enough for all the children we'll have,' I said, and her smile was so beautiful, so radiant, so pure and innocent.

'If only dreams could come true,' she said. 'I would bear you a hundred beautiful children. I love you, Saul, so very much.'

That last night in Watty's apartment ended up with few words more. What more was there really to say? I still clearly remember my last soft long kiss from Watty, the tears in her eyes, as she boarded the bus to Jakarta. She slipped the keys of her apartment into my hand.

'I don't need these, I've got my own,' I said.

'Better you take them, we've had a really good time there,' she said.

'This is no goodbye, Watty,' I said. 'You're getting me upset, so don't start this shit, OK! Remember what we talked about last night? When you get back from Jakarta we enlarge the apartment for the kids, OK?' I said, as I held her small hand in mine.

'Sounds great to me, Saul. Thank you for the love you have given me. I love you, Londo, I truly wish that we could stay together,' she said, as she headed off up into the bus. I watched her through the bus windows as she found herself a seat.

As the bus started to pull away I ran beside it. I pulled myself up to the window and yelled, 'Watty, Watty, Watty.' She moved over to the window and I shouted, 'I love you, I love you, that's why I didn't try to run, because I love you, so you came back, OK. I made myself a promise, I made myself a promise not to run, because I feel this way,' I said, still clinging to the moving bus.

Watty held the tops of my clinging hand and the tears started flowing from her eyes. She said, 'I love you, Saul, I love you too. I release you of your promise, I can never return to you.'

I ran alongside the bus, until it accelerated away in a cloud of fumes. I was sitting in the gutter with my chin in my hands when Bartak turned up.

'That's not the stand of a good cock,' he said.

'I'm not a good cock,' I replied.

'Come on, Saul, get up, let's go and have a drink. The world won't look so dim over the rim of a good glass of arak,' Bartak said.

For the rest of the day Bartak told me about his problems, but I could never tell him about mine.

As I sat and drowned my sorrows in arak, Bartak told me he was to be transferred to another prison and there was a new KPLP chief set to take his place. With Watty gone and my heart heavy, the time was right to find someone to take out my rage and despair on. I decided on my victim: the new KPLP chief.

I gritted my teeth for weeks while the new KPLP boss took over and he was a hard man. Of all the guards who could have been chosen to take over

KELL'S PRISONER

as the KPLP chief, it had to be Burri. He was nicknamed Talk Slow because of the way he questioned, and beat, the prisoners when they stepped out of line. Burri was a dog. His first decision as new chief was to stop the cockbreeding in Block F, then he stopped my exit passes. The fact that Bartak had come to visit me probably didn't help. Until he passed on a letter from Watty I'd been holding it together.

Her letter said, 'I don't hold you to your promise, Londo, life is too big for that. Do what you can to be free and I'll see you if all goes well. I am to have another operation on the 19th. Mr Bartak will tell you how it goes. I love you, Londo. Stay strong.'

After I read the letter I was fit to spew.

Burri was very jealous of Bartak and now that he had Bartak's job he wanted to be king. But his moment of glory was to be short lived. No sooner had he taken over the post as the head of the KPLP, than the first prison riots started.

CHAPTER 12

RIOT TO MAKE IT RIGHT

Do unto others
Before they do unto you

The riots began with a knife fight in Block Pusat, which was my block. The prisoners turned up the prison food box and beat up the kitchen trustees, who were fat and healthy buggers compared to the rest of the prisoners because of their free access to food.

Burri stomped down hard on the prisoners from my block. He sent the guards in with their truncheons, batons and nightsticks. The first riot started without any assistance from me, or any of my close mates. It started quite spontaneously over the distribution of rice. A prisoner named Ya Ya complained that his tin plate of food was only half full and when the trustee from the kitchen told him to piss off, Ya Ya got pissed off and threw it at him. Then he pulled out his knife, and that's when all the other prisoners in Block Pusat followed suit, beating the shit out of the kitchen trustees and turning up their food cart.

When my block was locked up, half the prisoners were thrown into the punishment block and the rest were handcuffed, beaten and thrown into their cells.

The following day the tension in the prison was as thick as Barry's farts on a bad day. Chook and I started to deliver the translation I had made of the Vienna Convention for the Treatment of Prisoners and that was the spark that a bomb factory is always in fear of. We passed out copies of the laws and regulations of the Indonesian prisons and the laws of Indonesia, which as basically an Islamic state and country stipulates, 'Every prisoner who doesn't have access to clean water will be issued with two buckets, one for his toilet and one for his wash, to cleanse himself before his prayers.' This bucket business really got them upset.

The second day after the riot passed tensely, as did the third and fourth days. On the fifth day Burri thought that all was back under control and he gave permission to open the huge steel gates that separated the blocks. That was his big mistake. If the blocks rioted separately, he could control them with the guards he had on duty as he only had enough guards to handle one block at a time. The prison was grossly understaffed. Once the prisoners from all the blocks were united, the story was very different. There was no way that the guards could control all of us. As soon as the blocks were opened up the next riot started. The prisoners went on an orgy of destruction.

Guards were cut, stabbed and killed with knives made up from bits of tin and old scrap metal from the workshops, sharpened pieces of wood, bone or even plastic. The prisoners not only turned on the guards, they turned on themselves, settling old feuds. I remember the Hit Man running up to me with a sharpened stick in his hand, laughing with half his hair burnt off his head and black soot on his face.

'We've just burnt down the wood shop, but I nearly got satayed – that's where I got this,' he said as he held up the sharpened shaft. 'Where next?'

This is what I had been building up, this is what I had been waiting for. This was the rebellion that Pak Mujiano was so terrified of and this was my cross and crown of thorns. The prisoners who trusted me, and put their lives in my hands, asked only, 'Where next?'

'The office and the front gate – if we can get into the prison armory, we won't need sticks. Get your best boys together and find Cop Killer and Thief,' I said.

'OK, but what do you want the Thief for?' he asked.

'Because that's just what he is. We need him and a couple of his boys, like Monkey Man and Fingers, to get up onto the main office roof and start pulling out the tiles, so that they can come in from the top of the roofs, while we go through the front and side doors and windows,' I said.

Off Hit Man ran, screaming and shaking his spear. When Cop Killer and the Thief turned up, they were wild. The riot had built them up into a frenzy. I couldn't control all the prisoners myself, but their leaders were my friends, they trusted me and took my advice. After all, it was the pamphlets that I had given to people like Hit Man, Cop Killer, Thief, Witchdoctor and a number of other prison gang leaders that got the whole ball rolling.

'OK, Cop Killer, remember how I showed you how to make firebombs? Take your boys into the kitchen and break into the storeroom where the *mynak tanna* [kerosene] is kept for the cookers. Remember to mix it with some petrol from the generator and make up as many firebombs as you can. Use every bottle, can, coconut or plastic bag you can find, and give half a dozen to Monkey Man and his mates. Thief, you get back here with at least a dozen for us, then you can go back to Monkey Man and his lot to show them how you can break in to a building from the top,' I said.

'Sure,' Thief beamed. 'They will need my experience once they're on the roof. Monkey Man can get on the roof, but he's still just a student, I can give him some valuable lessons for his future,' the Thief continued.

'OK, that's clear with you, Thief? Cop Killer, Killer of Dogs,' I said, as I placed a hand on Cop Killer's shoulder. 'Your job will be harder. What you've got to do, and it's the most important part of the plan to get out of here, we have to get control of the most deadly watchtowers and that's Towers 1 and 4, but if you can get some blokes together to also take out

Towers 2 and 3, then that will mean that we've got total control over the walls. If the police or army move in too fast, and we're all not long gone by then, well at least they will have to bargain with us,' I said.

'But how can I take control of the watchtowers?' Cop Killer asked, with a frown on his face.

'With your firebombs,' I said.

'But the guards are armed in the towers, they'll shoot us,' Cop Killer replied.

'Then burn the fuckers out!' I snapped, 'There's no more than nine bullets in every post, because that's all the guards are issued with, and how many of us are there? Over 800. Send in the arseholes first, and when their guns have run dry, fry the fuckers. The control of the towers means our life or death – if we're not successful today, tomorrow we'll all be dead.'

'We'll take the towers,' Cop Killer said, 'But once we're up there and the police and army move in, what do we do? Spit at them, or flash our arseholes at them.'

'That's where Hit Man and I come in. Your hitting the watchtowers will throw more confusion on the whole set up and hopefully draw some fire from the rest of us, though it won't be good for you. But it sure should give the Thief, Monkey Man and Fingers, along with their lot, time to get on the office roof and come in from the top, while Hit Man and his boys hit the place from all sides. If Hit Man and his eight ex-army boys and I can get into the armory, we'll win the day,' I said, as Cop Killer dashed off, clawing through the mayhem of prisoners calling out to this man or that.

As the burning smoke filled the air, I was confident that the people in the market who washed their clothes, bodies and vegetables in the creek next to the prison, were surely aware of what was happening inside the prison.

Time had become our worst enemy. As I broke from the crowd of rioting prisoners with Hit Man and his ex-army boys the guards started shooting. I watched as a group of over 30 prisoners tried to storm a post. One of the guards took aim and fired into the crowd, and when his rifle ran dry, firebombs engulfed him. He tried to put out the flames, but still more firebombs burst around him. As he fell over the watchtower post's railing he was holding his face and screaming, until he landed on the ground, then the prisoners set to him, chopping, stabbing and stoning him to death.

A volley of shots rang out from the prison office and half a dozen prisoners in the front ranks fell to the ground. I could see the Thief, Monkey Man and Fingers on the office roof with a good dozen other prisoners, ripping up the tiles and dropping in from the roof.

'Now,' I screamed, and a volley of Molotov cocktails hit the front windows of the office block, some busting on the outside walls, some breaking through most of the already broken windows and exploding in the offices. Flames were starting to appear from everywhere. The guard in Post 4 threw his rifle up into the air as the first attack of firebombs set his post alight, and jumped over the wall. 'Break your legs, you bastard,' I thought, as the prisoners made a human ladder. I watched as they used their own bodies as bricks, just as they had in Tower 1, to gain possession of the post. Once these were secure, I was confident that the same techniques would be used to get control of Towers 2 and 3. There were only four watchtowers on Madura, as compared with the seven watchtowers in Krobokan.

We were winning, it was costing heaps, but we were winning.

Now all we needed were weapons to fight with. I called Hit Man over and said, 'We've got to bust through those windows. Get all the rags you can get, and all the sarongs and shirts you can score off the other prisoners. We can wrap them around us, wet them well in this drain, then all together we go through those windows.'

Within minutes Hit Man and his team had commandeered enough cloth and rags to wrap us up, wetting everything in the drain first. I threw a glance at my bandaged bunch of mongrels.

'You all know where the armory is. Your rags are wet so if they catch fire, it's not your skin, so don't worry about it. Have you all a weapon of some sort?' I said, as I wrapped a rag around my head and face, and nine rag-covered faces all nodded at me, holding up an assortment of knives and double-ended pointed sticks. Hit Man still had his spear.

'OK, Hit Man, get them to throw another volley of firebombs through the windows. The minute they burst we all follow – straight through the windows, right?' I said.

When the next burst of firebombs sailed through the prison office windows, we charged through the broken and burnt frames, throwing our bodies into the flimsy wooden glass frames.

I clearly remember that once I got up from the drain, I yelled out '*Sekarang*,' and bolted towards the windows. Hurling myself at them with such force, it seemed like only match sticks I encountered. The demon was out, not only in me, but in all of us. Not one of them hesitated, those men were the equal of any Gurkha troops I've ever known. There was no lack of courage among any of them that day.

I rolled when I hit the floor and through the roll I could see a prisoner armed with only a sharpened stick attack a guard.

The guard shot him through the chest. I was still rolling, doing my best to get out of this guard's way, as he aimed his pistol, desperately looking around for something or someone to shoot.

The next thing I saw was Fingers falling to the floor, right at the feet of the guard. The guard pointed his pistol at Fingers, and was pulling the trigger for all he was worth, when up from behind him stood a smouldering pack of rags with a knife. I had just rolled under one of the tables as he came up behind the guard, who was so busy emptying his revolver into Fingers he had no idea. This smouldering pack of rags snapped the guard's whole head and face to the left, using his left hand, and with his right hand he pushed a knife all the way up through the guard's throat, pushing the knife deep up through the mouth and into the guard's brain. Then he gave a professional twist, so that the air could run into the wound, and once the air was in there could be no vacuum, which would make it easier to pull the knife out again.

As the guard dropped, I yelled, '*Ikut, ikut,*' (or 'follow me'), in Indonesian.

As we ran up the corridor leading to the armory room, two guards stepped out, one with a rifle and one loading his pistol. I leapt at the guy loading his pistol and as I threw myself through the air, bullets flew over my head. The guard who I had tackled went down to the floor and I rolled to the side. I could see the guard with the rifle still standing up, picking his targets and firing at them. I kicked up at the barrel to throw him off his aim and milliseconds later there was a bunch of rags on top of him, pushing a sharpened stick deep into his chest.

There was a God Almighty 'bang' in my ears and the guard who I had tackled started to shake and kick like a wild man. I was still holding his legs as I heard the clunk of his revolver hit the ground. When I looked up I could see a wooden pole sticking out of the guard's chest, with the Hit Man standing over it.

'You nearly got your head blown off then, Saul, you're lucky that I watch over you,' he said.

'So that's how stupid you are – better you watch over your family's ducks. Secure this corridor while we empty the armory,' I replied.

But the armory was a let-down. There were dozens of FN rifles and heaps of revolvers and automatics of all sorts, but no ammunition. Of all the fucking shit a bloke has to go through, we all battled like a horde of locusts to get to where we were, with the loss of three or more of my rag-bag friends. A million thoughts started to reel through my mind. Burri . . . Burri, of course, Burri – he's got the ammunition in the KPLP offices.

'Hit Man,' I yelled, 'We have to get into the KPLP office. These guns are useless without bullets. Keep the boys here, you stay here, we can't afford to lose the armory now. Give me one good man, and we'll do a roll straight out of here and back into Burri's office, OK?'

The Hit Man screamed out something I couldn't understand, and when I leapt back out of the window, the prisoners outside all screamed and cheered. I instantly turned around and made a leap back through another window into the KPLP office, followed closely by another rag-clad body bursting through the next window.

When I hit the floor in Burri's office I kept rolling until I hit the wall, then quickly stood up behind a tall grey filing cabinet. I had no sooner done that when I saw another rag-bag gain his feet. As he stood up holding his spear, I thought, Hit Man, you arsehole, and that's when Burri stepped out, shakily holding his revolver.

'So now I have you, Saul,' he said, pointing the gun at Hit Man, 'and now I can kill you.'

We were all wearing rags, not only over our arms and legs, but over our heads, faces and throats, to protect us from the fire and the sharp edges of the glass windows that we had to leap through. Burri couldn't have recognised me. I was the first to leap through the windows but Hit Man was so hot on my heels, Burri only heard one smash as the two of us crashed through into his office.

Burri pointed his gun and fired boom, boom, boom. Hit Man was lifted off his feet, his spear flew into the air and landed at my feet. Burri fired two more shots, but his revolver only went click, click. That's when I stepped out from behind the filing cabinet and picked up Hit Man's spear. All Burri could see were my eyes.

'Put that thing down,' he said, 'The Londo is dead.'

I just stood there looking at him.

'The Londo is dead. He's dead, he's dead,' Burri screamed, as he tried to reload his revolver.

'Don't waste your time, Burri,' I said, as the bullets in his hand started to drop to the floor. He stared at me, with a look of total disbelief in his eyes.

I held Hit Man's spear and said, 'This Londo's not dead, not by a long shot.'

When the sirens started to ring I knew that they were police sirens, not sirens of the prison. Then I heard the rifle shots. They couldn't be rifles used by the prisoners. The rifles in the armory had still not been distributed because we had no ammunition. When I looked out of the broken windows of the KPLP offices, prisoners were running everywhere, and tear gas shells were dropping down amongst the chaos of it all.

I pulled the rags over my face and nose more securely and leapt out through one of the windows leaving Burri behind in the mayhem and confusion.

When I gained my footing, I followed the rest of the prisoners, running as fast as I could, pulling off the rags that covered my face, head, arms and hands. As the tear gas shells fell, I managed to find my block. I was no sooner inside my block when armed police and soldiers rushed in firing indiscriminately into the running mass of prisoners. Most of the fleeing prisoners had to run through my block, Block Pusat or the central block, to get to blocks, A, B, C and D.

That's why my block was called Block Pusat, meaning 'central' in Indonesian, the other four blocks ran off it, two on one side, two on the other. As I found my cell, I could see the Chook and Plague's white faces looking at me, as they peeped through the bars of their cells, then disappear as they ducked their heads as a tear-gas container burst on the cement walkway running alongside our cells. I scrambled into my cell, closed the door, then did all I could do – I waited.

About an hour and half later, all the screaming and yelling died down, with the sound of the occasional shot here and there. I had cleaned myself up and changed my clothes. My mind was racing in a thousand directions, when the paramilitary soldiers opened my cell. My first thought was, 'They look like pissed off Pathat Lao. Will they shoot me in the cell or take me outside and do it?' I was fully expecting to die that day.

But then a guard pushed them away yelling, 'It's one of the foreigners, it's one of the foreigners, this is one of the foreigners' cells. Saul, Saul.' Just then one of the sweetest faces appeared – it was Doma, the little Christian donkey.

'What's happening Doma?' I asked.

'Barry and James have been locked up in their cells, I've got the keys here, there's been a lot of trouble in the prison. Food and water will be sent to you later, and the Director has ordered that guards be placed outside your cells,' he said, then left accompanied by those bad-arsed cranky-looking soldiers.

Well, I've just been given a reprieve, I thought, but for how long? A day, maybe two if I'm lucky. But when they know what I have done or what I am responsible for, what will they do to me then? Will they just come into my cell and shoot me like they were doing to some of the other prisoners just a couple of hours ago? But if they did that, how would they explain it? After all, the Chook and the Plague saw me dash into my cell. I suppose they could tell them that I tried to escape and that they had to shoot me. Then again they could just come in and bash me to death. But then the Chook's and Plague's cells were right next to mine. (The Italian, Guiseppe, had been transferred from Madura nearly a year before, because of complaints from his embassy, so there were only three foreigners on Madura, all Australians.)

The following day food and water was brought to us and the armed guards outside our cells were taken away. We could see the occasional prisoner dragged from his cell and taken up to the makeshift offices at the front of the prison for questioning. Some were dragged or carried back, a mess of bruises and blood, and some did not return.

On the second day, Barry was taken from his cell. When he returned, smiling and laughing with the guards, he was placed back in his cell; then the Chook was taken out of his cell and escorted to the front for questioning.

Once they were gone, I called out to Barry, 'Hey, Plague, what's happening?'

'Half the place is burnt down; that'll teach the bastards to build prisons out of wood. Maybe the Dutch had this all in the back of their mind, when they got them to build the shit pit, just in case they got locked up inside themselves? All the Londos had to do was get a box of matches and burn the fucking place down. They're talking about Londos, they think that one of us was involved, so I covered your arse, fuckwit. I told them that the three of us were in my cell from the beginning to the end, OK!' he said. 'So get that straight: you, me and Chook were in my cell the whole time, and if they ask you about those bloody pamphlets you made, you know nothing about them. All you did was help Hit Man with his English, that's all, you didn't know what he was up to. They asked me if I helped Hit Man and I told them, sure I did, whenever a prisoner wants to learn English, of course I'll help him with his words or study. So do you and Chook, but none of us knew what Hit Man was up to. Stick to what I've already told them, Russ, and there is nothing they can do, I hope,' he said, seeming uncomfortable.

'What about Chook? What do you think they'll do to him?' I asked.

'Well he's bound to get a few clips across the lugs. They didn't beat me because I've been here over three years longer than you two, so they trust me a bit. You both came here together, so they know you're close mates. All I could say to him, as he was taken out of his cell and I went back into mine, was, "Say nothing, you know nothing, insist on reading my statement before you make one yourself, you know my writing, they can't fool you," and then the Chook was marched off.'

I knew the chances of ever copying Barry's handwriting were nearly impossible, as his writing was like calligraphy. Barry had a special style of writing that would be difficult for any English scholar. It was nearly impossible to forge, and there were no English scholars where the questioning would be going down, or were there?

'So why have you put your neck out, Plague?' I asked.

'Because I know these people better than you think you do. They still haven't told the people outside what has happened in here. No one knows outside, and those who are smart will keep their mouths shut. Do you think our embassy will come to save us? You're a fuckwit if you do. The embassy, along with everyone else in this country, knows nothing of what's happened here. The three of us can die today or tomorrow, and all they have to say is that we died in the riot, and then produce a few burned bones to our government. I'm not trying to save you, you prick,

I'm trying to save myself, and to do that I have to save all of us, mate. Remember those five Australian journalists that the Indonesian soldiers knocked off? Remember, mate, they murdered five Aussie journalist citizens, and the Aussie government did nothing. If they kill us, the fucking embassy would probably pat them on the back. We know nothing about what went down; if we can't get out all together, then these bastards will make sure that none of us get out. One death is as easy to explain as three, so remember when the Chook gets back it's you next, and it's you that they're suspicious of, you fucking idiot,' he said, as I went quiet for a while, to gather my thoughts.

'Russell, Russ, Russ,' Barry called out to me, 'did I tell you that three guards were killed and four were badly hurt? Good one, the world's been made a better place.'

When the guards returned with the Chook, he was looking as fit as ever. As they locked him up in his cell and they took me out of mine, Chook clambered over towards the bars of his window, throwing out an arm with his thumb up in the air. 'Give 'em a Schultz, "I know nothing, I see nothing", way to go, way to go,' he said.

Yes I thought, but this ain't *Hogan's Heroes* and we ain't on TV: this is for real.

I was escorted to one of the lesser burnt-out offices and told to sit in a chair. The office was full of men, some in uniform and some in plain clothes. Barry had warned me about what to expect. There were people there from Indonesia's Intel and Luxus, which are the strong arm of Indonesia's Internal and External Intelligence, along with a Kodim man from the army, still in uniform, who headed the paramilitary strike force which hit the prison, cleaning it up and putting an end to the riot so quickly and professionally, not too mention so forcefully and so lethally. The local head of the Maduranese police in full regalia was also there.

As I sat on the chair, they all just carried on as if I wasn't there. One of the policemen came up to me and said in Javanese, 'Wrong chair, get out of it.'

I looked up at him and said, '*Apa?*', which is 'What?' in Indonesian. The people in the room looked at me, and then at the copper.

He kicked the chair I was sitting on and in Maduranese said, 'Wrong chair, get out of it, move,' and again I remained seated.

Looking up at him again, I said, 'Apa, Apa?'

The guard started to kick the shit out of the chair, breaking its legs. I fell to the ground.

'You motherfucker,' I yelled in English as I hit the floor. 'You dog-arsed snivelling cesspit,' I said still using English. '*Apa masalah? Apa masalah?*' I said, this time using Indonesian once again: 'What's the problem?'

The policeman backed off and I found myself sitting on the floor. When I looked up, everyone in the room was looking down at me, one of the civilian-dressed blokes came up to me and helped me from the floor.

'Please sit here,' he said, as he guided me to another chair. 'Would you like a cigarette?' he asked, using English.

'No thank you, I don't smoke,' I replied in English.

He smiled as he looked at me with ice-cold black eyes, like that of a snake sizing up its prey, saying in perfect English, 'Yes, it's a terrible habit I've not managed to break. What is your name?'

'Russell Kenneth Duparcq,' I replied.

'Yes, I know that. I also know the alias, or should I say the aliases you are known by. You really have been a busy man, a most industrious drug dealer and very diligent. If you weren't here serving a 20-year sentence in this prison, well, you could probably be doing anything you turned your eye to, and yet, you don't speak Maduranese or Javanese, very interesting,' he said, as he got up and left the room, leaving only a few policemen.

Most of the other people in the room had already left. As he walked out through the doorway, four soldiers entered the room, one holding a spear. As soon as they entered and closed the door behind them, I said nothing. I knew where the spear had come from.

I took my beating. The soldiers beat me with the spear, they yelled and screamed at me in Javanese, 'Tell us to stop and we will.'

When the spear was passed around, the soldiers began crying out in Maduranese, 'Tell us to stop and we will.'

But to cry out in any of those languages was to admit that I was involved in the riot, because the bulk of the prisoners involved in the riot could only speak Javanese or Maduranese. If I couldn't have spoken those languages, I couldn't have been involved, least of all be one of the ringleaders. All I could do was scream out in English or Indonesian.

'Pig fuckers, pig fuckers, your mothers wear your fathers' underpants, your sisters sell themselves for a good time, your grandmothers run whorehouses,' I yelled, and they nearly kicked the life out of me.

When those soldiers, and a couple of coppers who were involved in bashing me were called off, the little prick with the good English returned. I've learned to become very wary of most Asians who speak good English.

I was pulled up on a half-burnt sofa in the office and he said, 'You did quite well, you only used English, and a little bit of Indonesian today, but I am sure you knew what your tormentors were saying.'

'Your translations weren't as innocent as Barry claims. You knew what the prisoners here would do, that's why you passed these subversive translations around. An Indonesian prisoner would never think of taking the guard towers or the armory. They were the ideas of a foreigner, they were your ideas. Ideas formulated with you and your Australian friends, and I know I am right,' he said. 'Your subversive ways helped start all this trouble in my country,' he continued.

As I stared up at him I thought, 'Dear God, give me strength, give me strength, dear God, let me kill this bastard, dear God, let me save the lives of my mates with mine. If I can take this arsehole out, and I have to go with him, then so be it. But keep my mates safe, and, God, if you're really there, take care of my family, I love them all so very much.

As I set my sights on what could only have been a suicidal move, I slowly dropped my hand to the ground, where I had seen a long dagger-like piece of broken glass on the floor next to where I was now sitting. The piece of glass was to my right and all the soldiers and police were on my left talking with each other, not realising what I was about to do. I slowly picked up this razor-sharp piece of glass, which was a good nine inches long, and as I did it started to cut into my hand. I couldn't feel it cutting into my hand at the time, I felt only its warmth, the warmth of my own blood. I was somewhere else.

My mind seemed to become crystal clear, 'Don't die in vain, take as many as you can with you,' I thought.

The soldier standing beside me to the left was holding an M16 loosely in his hands, with the safety off. A past lifetime seemed to flash through my mind in milliseconds, as the gravelly voice of my former instructor took hold of me.

'M16, gas operated, air cooled, automatic, semi-automatic assault weapon, weighing 7.6 pounds, 20 round magazine, maximum range 2,350 metres, effective range 460 metres, automatic firing rate 650 rounds. That's what the factory says, but if you can keep them flying at a 100 rounds a minute, I'll be happy,' he cried, as we cut loose into the jungle, changing clips as quickly as our hands could manage, firing and rolling at all the targets set up on springs and strings to test us.

'Get the rifle,' I said to myself, as I clenched the long sliver of broken glass. 'Take out the soldier first.'

My mind had gone back to the land of hardened killers, where there is no tomorrow, only the moment of here and now. 'Kill them, kill them, kill as many as you can, kill them and justify your pain and suffering,' I thought.

Just as I was about to make my move and thrust myself into eternity, stabbing the soldier in the throat with this blade of glass and grabbing his rifle, it felt as if someone grabbed my hand in an iron grip. 'No, no, no, not now,' said a soft voice in my ear. 'Wait, I am with you.' It was a voice I thought I recognised . . . Watty!

Just then Mr Bartak broke into the office yelling out, 'I'll handle this, I'll handle this, I am the new temporary KPLP Chief until Jakarta replaces me. Where's Saul? Saul, Saul?' he said.

'I am here, Pak,' I said, but his voice was not the soft voice that I had just heard, it was not the one that had just spoken to me, telling me to wait.

Bartak pushed his way towards me through the guards, and when he saw where I was sitting he moved up and turned his back towards me, saying to the other people in the room, 'Russell is my prisoner, as too are the other two foreign prisoners, they are now my responsibility. Jakarta has cleared them from any involvement in these troubles and they are to be transferred to another prison. If you wish to question my authority then phone the Kanwil in Surabaya or Jakarta. You can leave this prison, and so can the rest of you. The prison guards can now safely take over the security of this prison. Thank you for your assistance,' he said to the befuddled Kodim officer.

As Bartak chased everybody out of the prison office, I was still peaking, trying to work out just what had happened. My mind was racing in a hundred different directions and none of them was good.

When he finally returned to where I was still sitting, he said, 'My government is not as bad as you think. Someone made a phone call yesterday telling them that you three foreigners were still alive and whoever made that phone call could always phone your embassy too, but it appears your embassy has still not yet been informed. What we've decided is to move you and to do that I've given my personal word that none of you was involved in this riot. If it turned out that one of you were, well it could cost me more than my job and position, is that clear, Saul?' he asked.

I looked at him and nodded.

'There are three of you at stake, Saul, do you understand that?' he said.

My eyes were still on his as I nodded again. He lit up a cigarette and stared at me. Once it was lit, he puffed on it and as the smoke cleared he looked down at my arm still hidden under the sofa, 'Show me your spur, Saul, show me what you would face death with.'

I paused for what seemed a very long time, then looking down my arm at my hand, I pulled out the long blade of glass from where I was hiding it. As I held it up the blood ran through my fingers.

Bartak didn't budge, he just stared at me and then slowly pulled a letter out from his pocket. 'If you want to kill me, Saul, there's no one in this office to stop you, I am just an old cock, my spurs have long since broken, but the way you hold that,' he said, nodding at the long sheaf of glass, 'reminds me of the great fights of Akbar and Fire, and now of Saul. Do you still lust for battle so much that you would face all those rifles with one spur?' he asked.

'No, Mr Bartak,' I said, as I dropped the glass on the floor, hearing it break into a hundred pieces, 'if it were anyone but you, I would never drop my spur, I would fight until it was broken or I lay dead, like all good fighters.'

'Dear Allah, if I were to have a son like you, I would count my life gifted,' he said, as he reached over from the table and took my blood-sodden hand.

He washed and cleaned my hand with a first-aid pack he took from a shoulder bag he had with him. The bag had a pistol inside it and he asked me to hold this bag while he dressed my wounds.

Bartak trusted me as much as my father would. He personally took me back to my cell, making sure that the Plague and the Chook were given water and food on the way.

When my cell was opened, he came in with me, saying, 'Swallow these with your water,' and he gave me a handful of tablets to swallow.

He stayed with me a good half hour, then asked how I felt.

'Sweet,' I said. 'My hand doesn't hurt any more, nor does my back where those fuckers kicked me.'

'Well that's good,' he replied. 'Now swallow these.' He gave me another handful of pills.

'And what's this for?' I asked. 'Where's the letter you promised to give me, you pulled it out in the office before and never gave it to me? So where is it?' I asked, feeling as loose as a dysentery attack.

'Swallow these antibiotics first and I'll give it to you,' he said.

I was so off my face with the tension of the day and all the pills he had given me, that before I had taken the rest I was on my back, sleeping like a baby.

When I woke up a couple of hours later it was cold and it was night. I rolled up in my sarong to get warmer. I tried to go back to sleep and finish the faraway dream I was having, but shots in the prison compound made me wake up and cleared my mind.

I dragged myself over to the prison bars and watched two policemen drag out one of the prisoners by the arms, with his feet dragging behind him. As they passed by my block, I was about to scream out something, but my mind started to clear a little more – the letter, what's in that letter? Maybe it's from the embassy? Or the Justice Department? Or maybe it's a copy of the order for our transfer? Whatever that letter was, it was our safe ticket out of here, I thought.

I finally found my matches and lit a candle. I pulled the letter out that had somehow nestled its way under my pillow, but first I had to rip open the envelope and that seemed to take me ages. Once I got that under control, a guard passed by asking me who had given me the candle, and when I told him that Mr Bartak had given it to me, the guard asked did I need more.

'Yes, please,' I said, 'and I'll slip you a thousand rupees if you get them quickly.'

Within seconds the guard returned with a pack of candles and a bottle of arak. 'Keep your money,' the guard said. 'Mr Bartak said that these are yours. If you need anything else, just let me know.' Then off he went again.

Shit, I thought, Bartak must think that I got rid of Burri for him and he's doing the right thing. After all, Burri had been backstabbing Bartak on every turn, and they hated each other's guts. Pak Bartak confided a lot in me at the cockfights over a couple of glasses of arak and on a number of occasions he had told me that his job was made hard because of the stealing of the prisoners' food by the prison director and the head of the kitchen, Burri and Darmorrow. How could Bartak improve this place with Burri, especially, ripping off everything, even the lepers' medicine? No there's no love lost there, I thought.

I lit up half a dozen candles to chase away the dark and cold and finished opening the letter. The smell that came out of it was of a special fragrance that only two people who know each other well would ever recognise. Watty, I thought, it's got to be Watty.

When I opened the envelope, it had within it a small collection of my own letters and notes that I had given to her. All of which she generally kept with her and all of which seemed to have absorbed her aroma. Why were they sent back to me?

The next envelope explained. It was from a friend of hers, who had sent me a letter informing me that Watty had passed away and that she had asked this friend to return these letters to me via Pak Bartak.

I guess the Angel of Death delivers her mail in many ways, but collects it in only one.

That was the day my heart turned to stone. That night I slept very little and those sleepless nights continue to this day.

As life or death would have it, after the riot I was transferred to another prison in the central highlands of Java called Malang. Malang in Indonesian means 'adversity, misfortune or unlucky' and I spent the next six years of my life there.

The Spaniard died in my arms in Malang. He was the only other surviving white man I knew there, he was my friend and comrade, and he died in my arms, amid the filth and squalor of a third-world prison cell.

I managed to send flowers to his grave and also to Watty's.

I am alone now. The last white man in this world.

Who will put flowers on my grave?

CHAPTER 13

AND THE ANGELS WEPT

A winter's heart is only as cold
As the owner will allow it to become

Malang, October 1994. This is my fifth year in this prison – or is it my sixth . . . I must have served at least nine of those years by now, I thought to myself as I turned on my radio . . . It was a very quiet and still night. The reception was excellent . . . I heard an Australian broadcast and as I did I felt a hollowness in my heart . . . The voice of the female English speaking commentator pulled at my heart and spirit. I wanted to go home . . . I imagined this female commentator with fair hair, white yet creamy skin and with big blue eyes . . . an image I had to wipe quickly from my mind to survive. Prison had taught me that loneliness and depression were every bit as deadly as a disease or a dagger.

With over three years of solitary confinement under my belt, I knew what loneliness was. The years I spent without speaking my mother tongue, English, the years I spent without seeing my own face, let alone seeing the face of a fellow white man, have taken their toll. I know what loneliness is. The psychological torture, the physical torture, the nutritional deprivation, the sleep deprivation, these are an easy burden to carry, an enemy I know well. But the hardest thing for me to handle was the loneliness. I missed my family, my own people, the people of my homeland Australia.

Around me, all I saw were dark, secretive faces, among whom I must stand, I must live, I must survive.

The assassins of Makkassar were as feared in the prison as the plague itself. If there was any crime that they had not committed, the only reason would have been that the opportunity hadn't presented itself. They were Muslims and they were cold, cold killers.

I first met them in Parmakasan Prison, but it was little more than a nodding acquaintance. I acknowledged their existence, and they acknowledged mine. These assassins were seven in number, their leader was a man named Mariso, who stood about five foot three inches tall and weighed about 55 kilograms. He had over 14 murders up his sleeve, along with various tattoos and a knife or two. When Mariso and his gang of cutthroats were first transferred to Malang, they had to assert their status and set their position amid the prison hierarchy.

All seven of them would take over the food carts and take what they wanted from them, leaving their scraps for the rest of the prisoners in their block. Now this was no concern of mine, I was in a single cell in Block D. I acquired this cell through corruption and bribery, as did the other 30 or so prisoners who shared my block.

I was a pumuka, a form of trustee or boss, for the small church we had in the prison. Part of my job was to keep the church clean, not to mention stop the Islamic prisoners from stealing the Bibles and using them to start their cooking fires. So as long as the assassins were only terrorising their own block, and didn't hassle me or my position on top of the shit heap, I didn't give a fuck about who they killed, bashed, raped or robbed.

Over the months, the gang built up a formidable reputation for ruthlessness. They even killed two of the prison gang bosses, leaving a vacuum in the gang leadership, which Mariso quickly took advantage of and filled with his own cronies. Thus his gang became bodyguards for the two new gang leaders.

Eventually the inevitable happened. Pieta, the younger brother of Mariso, came into my cell one morning and stole my daily ration of food. It was not enough to live on by any means, but it was enough to help me survive. If I were to let them steal from me once, it would never stop. They would start small, until every pitiful possession I owned was in their hands and all my food was in their bellies.

I had no choice, so I went after Pieta. I discovered him in another block, not his own, but a block where I had friends, so I kicked the shit out of him. When he pulled a knife I, to my amazement, managed to get it off him very easily. I can clearly remember standing over Pieta with the knife in my hand, looking down on him, as he was crying and trembling. The fear that came out of him, you could not only see, but you could practically taste it and I thought, 'You're just a piece of paper, without your friends here, you're just a blank piece of paper.'

The other prisoners in the block at the time gathered around, and tried to gee me up to kill Pieta, by screaming, '*Bunnu, bunnu, darah, darah,*' or 'Kill him, kill him, blood, blood.' As their endearments started to pick up – '*Bunnu, bunnu, darah, darah*' – Pieta's sarong darkened, as his urine flowed freely across the floor. He looked like such a pathetic creature. I just gave him a few good kicks, to add insult, and called him an *anjing bungsut,* or a low-life dog.

As I left that block and returned to my own, word of the fight got around the prison like the clap in a whorehouse. Soon the assassins were to find that they were the object of a lot of jokes and ridicule, as the white man, Saul, had kicked the arse of one of the assassins. Too add even further insult to their injuries, he took the knife off Pieta, the assassin, and refused to even cut Pieta a little, so he had no scar to show and prove how hard he had fought. He had lost face.

If I had cut Pieta, even just a quick slash across the face, chest, arms or legs, anywhere that would have drawn blood, things wouldn't have been as bad as they were. But no blood, no scar, no face, was the code of the assassins. The outcome of this fight had caused a loss of face, and the only way that face could be regained was with my death, the death of Saul.

During my years in Malang I had made a lot of friends, both prisoners and guards, and the name Saul was the only name that I would answer to. The following day, after the fight with Pieta, I was in my cell doing something or other when I heard a lot of yelling and screaming outside. I looked out of my cell door and I could see the prisoners running towards the gate, running out of my block as some other prisoners were pushing their way in.

The first one I recognised was Mariso, then Pieta, then of course, the rest of the assassins. They took up their positions, letting everyone run out of my block, then started to walk down the empty block towards me. The ones on the right and left started to fan out. I could see they all had their stomachs tightly wrapped with strips of cloth, to protect their vital organs and stop their stomachs from dropping and falling out should they get slashed across the abdomen in a fight. They also had headbands tied around their foreheads to keep the hair out of their eyes, and in their hands they carried an assortment of knives.

I had nowhere to run . . . nor would I have, if the chance to run were at all possible. No, there is a reason I'm here, and maybe it's to teach you fuckers a lesson, or vice versa, I thought.

OK, you scumbags, this is as good a day to die or live as any, but if I am to die I won't die alone. I quickly looked around the prison yard where I was, looking for anything to fight with, a stone, a handful of sand, a stick, and yes, there was a long pole attached to a makeshift mop. I grabbed the stick, and kicking down with my right foot, I snapped the mop head off, then ran full pelt at the assassins, spinning the stick above my head.

The last thing that they were expecting was for me to attack them first.

God was with me on that day, as I guess he has been with me on many other days. I had studied the lathi in India – it is just a long pole about one and a half metres long, and if you know how to use it, it is the most formidable of innocent-looking weapons. The lathi was about as inconspicuous as an old man's walking stick, or a shepherd's staff, but deadly beyond belief in the hands of a trained man, woman or child.

I smashed into these assassins with the speed of a cat, like a man truly possessed, possessed with the will to live at any cost. I was determined not to die alone, not if I could possibly help it.

The fight was hard, and as I said, very very fast. Incredibly, within the first minute of their entering my block I managed to incapacitate three of the assassins. The other four, led by Mariso, bolted when they saw how quickly their mates went down.

I was hyped beyond control and running on pure adrenalin as I chased after them in a screaming rage. Anger can be a scary thing, but it can also be a good ally.

I pursued them out of the block and ran straight into a dozen or so guards doing a rear wall guardpost change. I got into a bit of shit over this, but nothing that a couple of packets of cigarettes couldn't fix. After the fight, other prisoners started to come to me and ask me if I would teach them how to use the lathi for their own defence.

The gang bosses came to me for advice, or just to talk, and many of the prisoners of standing found prestige from my presence.

One day old Pak Minto, an aged and pleasantly plump Chinese prisoner said to me, 'If the other prisoners seek you out constantly to talk to you, or to be near to you, never get angry or cranky with them. It's not only because you are a stranger, a foreigner here, but you are to them like a window, a window to the world . . . and thus you become important to them.'

I guess to some I was a friend, I was important. To others I was an enemy. The years in Malang had changed me in many ways. I started to question life, and the reason for it, I questioned my own importance, my own worth.

I've read the Christian Bible five times, from cover to cover. I've read the Koran al Koran, the holy book of Islam, the Talmud and the Torah, the scriptures of the Hebrews, the holy book of the Jews. I've studied the teachings of the Buddha, and read from the rare Tibetan manuscripts, *Life of the Enlightened One* and the *Hindu Bagwan Gita*.

I searched for an answer in all the major religions of the world and found only more questions. My work in the church was not because I was a dedicated Christian – in all truth it started off as a profitable perk. I could get my mail smuggled in and out through the church, and I could arrange for needed medicines for myself and other prisoners, both Christian and Muslim alike.

During this period, when I was boss of the church, I met this incredible Chinese lady named Yani Lim. She had devoted her life to Christianity and leading by example. She fasted for sick prisoners and went without herself, to help the prisoners inside Malang Prison.

She told me that she couldn't convert a Muslim to Christianity, under threat of a prison sentence. I was pretty amazed when I was told about some of her Christian friends and how they were persecuted for their beliefs and attempts at spreading the Christian word. When she mentioned that one of the Muslim prisoners wanted to read the Bible, and had asked her for one, she told me that if she were caught giving Bibles away to Muslim prisoners, she would surely get into a lot of trouble with the prison administration.

'Let me give it to him,' I said. 'How can they put me in prison, when I'm already here?' And so it was that I started spreading God's word through the prison.

Many of the prisoners couldn't read or write, so I started to teach them, using the Bible. I told myself that this was only a display of rebellion towards the system of things within the prison and I guess within the country itself.

If it wasn't allowed, I wanted to do it.

After a cholera epidemic, my popularity within the prison soared to new heights. At its height, 22 prisoners died within one week. Nearly 200 lay side by side on the floor of the prison infirmary block. The first time I actually went into the block, to take some food into a Christian friend of mine who was sick, I discovered that the guards and trustees had deserted them all for fear that they might catch the disease and die themselves.

The sick were left to die on the ground where they lay; they had no boiled water and little or no food. Some were left to lie in their own excrement, others in their own urine, vomit or bile. I bribed the kitchen prison guard with cigarettes and money to arrange clean water and some extra food for the sick.

No one was game to carry this boiled water or food into the infirmary, or the cholera block as it was then called, so I did it. I felt good inside for what I was doing. I knew the prisoners really needed me or at least someone from outside the infirmary to help them and give them hope that they weren't just locked up and forgotten, left to die, which I had seen on so many occasions. I managed to knock off, or score through a dozen different brown hands, water, food, blankets and medicines.

The only other thing these blokes needed, apart from hope, was faith. The faith that they would survive. To Christian and Muslim alike I said, 'Faith, have faith, mate. If not in your Christian or your Muslim gods, then in yourself. Have faith in yourself. All things are possible if you truly believe in yourself and have the faith that you will live, and mate, you will live. Don't give up,' I preached, 'don't ever give up.'

The amount of prisoners who were dying slowed down, until eventually, the epidemic stopped.

For my efforts, I earned the gratitude, the respect, the friendship and the loyalty of not only prisoners, but many of the guards. The thought of catching cholera myself and dying, never entered my head.

Not long after the cholera outbreak subsided I woke up the worst way a man can be woken. At 06.00 on 7 October 1994, the assassins managed to get themselves out of their cell and into mine. They were all armed with knives and carrying murder in their hearts.

The first real thing that registered that morning was the pain in my left eye. The knife that caught me in the far side of the left eye was a hook-shaped knife, used to run up the side of cane and cut the off-shoots from the main stem. This blade was sharpened on both sides, so it went in easy, pulling my left eye out of the socket when it was withdrawn.

There were five assassins in my cell, all yelling and screaming and stabbing at me in a frenzy. Another two had knives at the throat of Ngadimun, my room boy, further out in the block. Lying on the ground, I started kicking, trying to defend myself, then Mariso jumped on top of me, desperately trying to pin my shoulders down. I saw his hand rise, with a knife firmly held in his white-knuckled fist.

Our eyes locked for a split second, then his eyes flicked down to my chest and instantly it was like a voice that screamed out, 'Your heart, your heart.' He was lining me up for a death blow. I desperately pulled my torso to the left and at the same time, I slapped at his right hand, as it came down towards my heart.

I managed to knock his hand off target, but not enough for him to totally miss me. The blade sunk deep into my chest, piercing my right lung, and the force of the hit knocked the wind out of me. I felt myself gasp and, as if a volcano were bursting inside of me; the rage flared up like nothing I'd ever felt before.

I reached up and grabbed Mariso by the face, sinking my fingers into his eyes and my thumb up into his mouth, between his teeth and the cheek of his face, and grabbed hold for all I was worth.

'I'll kill you,' I faintly remember growling, like a maimed predator.

My left hand was still holding his right hand, which in turn was still holding the knife that was buried up to the hilt in my chest. The fire of anger surged through me, the injured animal's rage took hold of my body, and as Mariso tried to pull away from my death grip, he actually helped to pull me to my feet.

Once on my feet, all I wanted to do was to kill them all. Give no quarter, ask no quarter. I could see the fear on their faces as I stood up. Mariso managed to pull his hand, and his face, free from my grip. I leant against the wall, for a second or two and that short pause gave me time to gather my thoughts and plan my attack – for attack was all I could do.

I must have looked a grim sight, with my left eye hanging out on my cheek, covered in blood from so many vicious and numerous wounds. Revenge . . . revenge, was all I could think of. 'Get the fuckers, kill the dogs, kill them all,' a wild frenzied little berko voice screamed from within my very soul.

Like the dickhead that I am, I pulled the knife out from my chest and screamed, in pain from pulling out the knife, and even more so from the anger, 'I'll take you all with me to fucking eternity,' I swore, as I ran at them.

They all turned and bolted from my cell and out of my block, with me in this insane pursuit. I guess I followed them for about 40 or 50 metres, then I slowed down and dropped to my knees. My head started to go all fuzzy. When I looked down at my naked chest, I could see bubbles of air coming out of my chest wound, along with a small fountain of pumping blood. My left side was aching and as I slowly turned to look behind me, all I could see was a river of blood, leading back to my cell.

My head started to ache, as if half of my skull was exposed to the world. Dropping the knife, I put my hands up to my face and I could feel this lump of something odd in the palm of my left hand. I gently pushed on it and passed out from the pain and the loss of blood. It was only on that short fall to the dirt that I realised that what I had felt in my hand was my own eye.

I was attacked at 06.00 in the morning, I was sent to an outside hospital in Malang at 07.00 hours and, after two hours of Indonesian doctors' attention, I was declared dead at 09.00 hours.

My body was sent to the morgue.

The prison authorities were informed of my death by the hospital, and a death certificate was issued and sent to the prison that same day.

The white Christian prisoner, Saul . . . was dead.

CHAPTER 14

'SAUL, SAUL, SAUL'

A man doesn't have to be born a king
To walk a king's path

Where am I? Where is this place? My mind seems foggy, yet somehow crystal clear.

I looked around me, recognising hundreds of things instantly, yet others I knew not what they were. I was standing in the middle of a large room, paint was peeling off the walls, which were stained and dirty. The lights were a mixture of fluorescent tubes, bulbs and natural light, coming in from an open window, whose glass panes were opaque, old and grey. Lined up against the wall were trolleys, hospital trolleys, with sheets covering the tops of them. Protruding from the rear end of these trolleys, poking out from beneath the sheets, were feet.

On each trolley there lay a body, and tied to the big toes of their feet were little tags . . . dead men's toe tags.

As I slowly surveyed the room, and all of the bodies, I noticed that their feet were dark . . . all but two. The two feet sticking out from under the sheet on that trolley were white. I moved closer to read the name, the name on this white man's toe tag, but I knew what it would read before it was really visible. I knew who it was before I even looked at the bottom . . .

Anger built up inside me . . . 'NO, NO, NO, I won't die, I will not die,' I screamed to myself, and at God, and yes, even the Devil.

'NO . . . I will not die now . . . not yet . . . NO,' I repeated, with all the conviction and belief that I would not die.

The next thing I remember was a giant gush of pure whiteness engulfing me, swallowing me and taking me away.

'NO,' I screamed at the whiteness, 'NO, I cannot go, NO, NO.'

I felt like I was fighting this whiteness, then boof, whoosh. White consumed me, then cold, so cold. I was lying in my body and it was so cold, it didn't seem like my body at all. It seemed like I was lying in a block of ice, the cold wasn't painful, it was numbing, but a far from pleasant numbing. It was fear.

I could hear people moving around me. I could hear them talking. I could feel the sheet pulled off my body when some medical students came into check on the dead white man. None of them had ever seen a dead white man before, and they were fascinated that the blond hair on my head was pretty much the same as my pubics.

I couldn't move . . . I couldn't speak . . . I couldn't cry out, 'I'm alive . . . I'm alive', and I so desperately wanted to, with all my heart, my soul and my spirit. I wanted to scream out to the world, 'I AM ALIVE!'

A fear was in me now, like I had never felt in my life . . . no, existence . . . ever before felt or experienced, for I knew where I was.

I was in the morgue.

Whoof, whoosh, the whiteness took me again. I was lost in its comfort once more. The whiteness took me away for a while, away from the cold . . . the ice . . . the fear . . . the pain . . . and the loneliness that follows death.

Then the ice returned, and with it the fear, the cold. I knew that I now lay in my body, as cold and lifeless as it was, or seemed, and as badly mutilated as it was, it was the only body I had . . . the only vessel to carry me to the end, and I didn't want to leave it . . . not yet.

I again felt the sheets pulled back, and instantly felt the warmth of Yani's presence. My little Chinese Christian lady, I knew that she would come. It seems that for some reason, I was waiting for her. I had to show her something. I had to prove to her that her faith in me was not wasted. When Yani arrived at the morgue she came in with the coffin for me to be buried in, and a few friends to help clean and wash my body, and to assist her in giving me a decent Christian burial.

These ladies washed my body, while Yani washed my face. She wiped the congealed and hardened blood from my right eye. When she stopped wiping my face, I could sense her looking at me, no I could more than sense her, I could see her, as if through a thin veil. I could see the tears in her eyes swelling up, then gently falling from her eyes and rolling down the soft porcelain skin of her cheeks. She picked up my hand, and holding it in both of hers, she started to pray. I became lost in her prayer, and seemed to be swept up in a dream, a sweet gentle dream.

When I felt a splash like hot water I couldn't comprehend where it was coming from. Something about me had changed. Warmth somewhere in my body, I felt warmth. The warmth of life.

Where is it? Where is this warmth coming from? Then I felt it on my right inside wrist.

Splash. Splash. Then again splash, so hot it seemed at first, so hot, then warming, splash, splash.

My whole essence seemed to centre around Yani's tears, splashing on my wrist, and this incredible distant, yet close warmth. What is it? Where is it coming from? The tears, I can see them, Yani's tears, Yani, Yani.

Her tears were falling from her cheeks and I could see them, each one individually falling down, down, down, to where they fell upon my right wrist, splashing, splashing, splashing.

The warmth, the warmth is life, I thought. The ice, the ice is death.

As I could feel the warmth slowly creep up my arm and reach my right armpit, I could hear Yani still praying. I became more intent on her words, I wanted to say something to her like, 'Of course I believe in God, Yani, and He knows that.'

'Please return your servant, Lord, there's so much, yes so much work he can do, and has done, even if he doesn't know it himself,' Yani pleaded with . . . God, I guess.

I felt that the room was crowded, and that Yani was pleading my case with someone who was just standing on the other side of me. Yani kept repeating the same thing for what seemed ages, but the cold got colder. It seemed that I was locked in a world of ice, freezing.

'I'm freezing, God I'm freezing, it's so cold,' I thought. Then like an afterthought it struck me, my arm, my arm was so warm, all under my armpit was starting to warm up. Then it was as if the heat had suddenly set a warm fuse to all the other tubes and cables, or veins and arteries, or whatever.

The warmth was life.

The warmth started to fill my chest, then my neck, my legs and arms. It was like someone had just given me a mild electric shock. I gasped, small though it be, and as faint as it was, it was enough, enough to catch Yani's attention.

She looked at me, her eyes lit up with hope and wonderment as she leapt to her feet and yelled, 'Praise the Lord . . . Doctor, doctor, Russell is alive. Doctor, doctor, he's alive, this man is not dead.'

An Indonesian doctor was found, and after arguing with Yani, he checked my heart with a stethoscope.

Finding no heartbeat, he said, 'I'm sorry, *Ibu* Lim [meaning Mother Lim], he is dead, and has been dead for over five hours.'

'No, he's not,' argued Yani. 'He's alive, I know it, God told me. He's not dead. Please check him again, or I'll bring in another doctor.'

The doctor grudgingly checked again, this time he searched for a pulse in my neck. When he found it, he nearly shat himself. 'Darah, darah,' he screamed, 'Cepat, cepat!' 'Blood, blood, get him out of here! Quickly, quickly.'

They rushed me to the operating theatre, and Yani found a Chinese Christian doctor, who was on holiday from Singapore, to spend eight hours of his time sewing me up, after he threw away all the damaged bits and pieces inside of me.

When I eventually left the hospital I was missing 80 centimetres of intestine, half a right lung, a gall bladder, my spleen and I was totally blind in my left eye.

Remarkably, I survived the operation without any antibiotics or painkillers. The hospital stay sucked, though, and I can tell you this, you have never experienced pain until you wake up from a deep sleep, after a serious intestinal operation, straight into NO PAINKILLERS . . . AGONY.

The prison wouldn't pay for the painkillers, or the antibiotics, and I had no money on me to buy them. The police guards wouldn't let Yani give me money, or leave me with any medicine. An Australian Embassy official told me that they couldn't lend me any money because all their petty cash and slush-fund money had been used elsewhere.

The medicines would have cost about $A100. Even in diplomatic circles life is cheap.

During my stay at the Malang Hospital I was under police guard due to my escape record and a number of other things that were noted. The police thought that I was a top candidate for a bolt, should the chance arise.

The police also told me that because a death certificate had been sent to the prison I was no longer a prisoner in Malang, or Indonesia for that matter. In order to hand me back over to the prison guards they had to cancel the death certificate.

On the ninth day my leg was unshackled from the rusty old iron hospital bed and I was, finally, officially handed back over to the regular prison guards. I guess it took them that long to get a 'Still Alive Certificate'. When I was handed over I was escorted straight back to the prison.

When I arrived, I was met by the prison director along with all the heads of offices within the prison. They were all really happy to see me, with genuine smiles I didn't realise they possessed. They all insisted on shaking my hand. Old Delrice, the head of the infirmary, popped out of the crowd of guards pushing a wheelchair for me, but I refused. He had a big round smile on his bronzed shining face and seemed tickled pink to have his translator of medicine bottles and tablet boxes back.

When word of my return spread around the prison, prisoners started to run up to the office to see if it were true.

'Has the white man Saul really come back from the dead? No, that was impossible,' they all thought.

The prison trustees, working in the prison offices, had seen with their own eyes my death certificate. So too had most of the guards. As far as the prison was concerned I was dead and the director kept it that way – for security reasons, I later learned.

Yet now this dead man had come back and very few could believe their eyes. As the large inside doors opened and the sun burst through to where I was standing, the prisoners started to flock into the building entrance, but the guards pushed them back. The director called out for extra guards and ordered them to push their way though, which they did.

Delrice, once again, offered me the wheelchair but again I declined. I could feel a strength building up in me as I looked at the laughing and smiling faces of the other prisoners.

I could hear them calling my name, 'Saul', and trying to talk to me over each other or trying to attract my attention: 'You no dead, Saul, hey! Saul no dead, *arsik, arsik*,' they yelled ('fantastic, fantastic').

Then from another direction, another bronzed beaming face smiling like a delighted child at a carnival, also tried to attract my attention, and screamed, 'Hey look, Saul live, Saul no can die, no can die, Saul no can die.'

As I stepped towards the open door, all of the prisoners stepped back and the guards slipped in between them in an arrowhead configuration forcing them to part. More prisoners were running up to the main road of the prison toward the offices. As their numbers began to swell into the hundreds, the guards were well and truly outnumbered.

I paused at the entrance of the door for a moment, which seemed like an age, as thoughts flashed through my mind. I squared my shoulders, and thought, 'I must walk all the way to my cell, I must not fall, I must not limp, or show weakness, and above all, I must not show the pain, I must not let them know how much I hurt. I must remember, I am not weakened by this, I am strengthened.'

As I lifted my head, I made eye contact with what seemed like well over a hundred prisoners and guards. In all of their eyes I saw respect, and in some, even admiration. As I tried to look each prisoner in the eye, I made contact with old Pak Minto.

His face was beaming with joy and I heard him yell out at the top of his voice, 'Jesus Christ came back from the dead in three days, you took nine days . . . you're six days late, so you're not a god.'

'No, no, he's not a god,' Suraji screamed. 'He's Saul . . . Saul . . . Saul.'

'Saul, Saul, Saul,' Pak Minto joined in with the chant.

Then other prisoners picked up on it, 'Saul, Saul, Saul.'

I stepped out from the doorway and started my way towards my cell, which was a good 400 metres away. As I walked down the long central road of the prison, the guards made a pathway for me, interlocking their arms to hold back the mass of prisoners who all seemed to want to touch me.

The prison came to a standstill and other prisoners came running from the workshops, kitchens, laundries and all of the other blocks.

They lined the road where I walked, over 2,000 men screaming and yelling one word in unison, 'Saul, Saul, Saul.'

Even the guards joined in with the cheer of 2,000 voices.

This thundering crescendo could be heard outside the prison until eventually cars started to beep their horns, bicycle bells rang and truck and bus horns sounded. As I walked that 400 metres back to my cell, the roar of sound that carried my name gave me strength.

The rumbling cry of 2,000 of the world's hardest and most lethal men . . .

All with one word on their lips:

'SAUL, SAUL, SAUL . . . SAUL, SAUL, SAUL . . . SAUL, SAUL, SAUL.'

WHEN NIGHTMARES END

God of the sea . . . I beg you . . . punish Ulysses,
visit him with storm and shipwreck and sorceries
let him wander for many years before he reaches home
and when he gets there
let him find himself forgotten . . .
Unwanted . . .
A stranger
(Homer, *The Odyssey*)

6 SEPTEMBER 2001.
This morning I opened my eyes slowly, without moving. I felt the warmth of the bed, smelt the soft sweet sleepy smell of the sheets and pillows and I reminded myself where I am . . . I am at home and I am free!

I hear the tinkle of a cup of coffee being made in the kitchen, by my girlfriend, and I thank God for all His blessings.

On the 26th of this month, I will have been free from prison five years. I close my eyes and I can remember, as clear as if it was only yesterday, that other life, that other world, that other person, who once dwelled within me.

The smells, the odours and aromas, the sounds of keys being rattled, the moans, the grunts and groans, all of another world flood back to me each day, in their own subliminal ways. Sometimes they come back to me in my dreams, in the dark of night, the screams and yells, the barked orders, the rancid reek of decay, rot, and blood.

I had been kicked awake one morning and was told that I was wanted in the prison security office. I had discovered that being kicked awake was a far better way to start the day than being stabbed awake!

The authorities had transferred me from Malang Prison the previous year after I'd spent nearly a year in solitary confinement after the stabbing – for my own protection, I was told.

This was after one of the prisoners who had stabbed me was found dead in his cell, with a bamboo stake pushed through the roof of his mouth and up into his brain. The culprit was never caught.

Where ever I go I seem to attract outcasts. My following in Jakarta's Tunggerung Prison were two Nepali prisoners, both doing life sentences; one mad Dutchman, serving four years; a Burmese student rebel, doing life; and an Irian Jayan Christian prisoner, called Jacob, serving seventeen years.

Each one of these men would split his last grain of rice with me and each one of them would stand beside me, in fights or riots and I beside them.

Christian, the mad Dutchman, could swing a rack of steel bed frames in a blue better than Conan the Barbarian could swing his sword. He was as strong as a horse, with a heart that was bigger and he looked like a half-crazed bubble-eyed Viking. He would become even more fearful looking the closer you got to him. He had what he called 'Stab them within a metre look!' I fear he may be madder than me.

Prem and Ram, the Nepalese, slept at my feet for months after I had suffered a stroke, caused by a blood clot I received when I was stabbed in the eye. This stroke hit me nearly a year after the initial injury. It took me about a month to shake off the effects of the stroke and regain the use of my right side, which I did by drinking Cobra blood. It seemed the only medicine that worked. I could not fight or fend for myself during this period and my survival prospects plummeted.

I had no family or embassy so to speak, to help feed, or wash, or defend me, within the prison walls. But I was blessed with the friendship of these men. They were my family.

When I was told to go to the security office that morning Dutchie put up some objection. 'One of those pricks could have set you up mate,' he said with a concerned look. Squatting down and speaking in a lowered voice he added, 'Those fights last week aren't all over by a long shot. Those visiting room trustees are all armed up, to fight with the kitchen trustees and just your luck you will get caught up in the guts of it.'

'Yeah,' said Prem. 'We better all go with you, mate. Don't want you dying without us,' and then he laughed a big open-mountain laugh, showing all his perfect white teeth. Prem was the son of a Veteran Gurkha soldier.

Prem had grown up in army camps throughout the world and his loyalty and strength, his devotion and trust, were beyond question to all of us. I have lived, worked and fought with Gurkha soldiers, who are without doubt the *best* soldiers in the world today, and Prem carried all the hallmarks of his father . . . of a Gurkha. He was only twenty-five years old, and already he'd spent four years in prison.

As it turned out I didn't have to fight my way to the prison security office or back from it. When I got to the office, I was informed that I was to be given a presidential pardon.

I couldn't believe my ears. I must've asked the guard a dozen times to repeat what he had been told to tell me by his superiors . . . That I have a presidential pardon exonerating me and setting me free . . . Free! Something I could never really believe until I finely set foot back onto Australian soil.

Saying farewell to my friends in the prison was very difficult. I only wished that I could have freed them too. As rough and tough as all those buggers may have been, there was not a dry eye when I bid them farewell.

My return to Australia was difficult for a number of reasons; I had to basically re-learn English, along with many words as I was constantly mixing my languages together. Indonesian and words from other languages seemed to constantly jump into my everyday English conversation. Many people must have found me irritating, I know it sure pissed me off.

I felt like a caveman who hadn't had a shower for over a decade. Actually, the grim fact was . . . I was a caveman and I hadn't had a shower for over a decade. (They don't have showers in Indonesian prisons.)

The plane trip back to Australia was like a dream. I don't think I spoke to anyone on the flight. My family was waiting for me, but they all seemed so old, so different.

I brought back with me an image of how things would be, but what I had imagined was very very different to what was reality.

My country had changed. Streets had changed, cars had changed, clothes had changed and cash had changed. Mobile phones, computers, microwaves and CD players weren't around when I was last in Australia. Nothing was the same as I remembered it.

My wife remarried seven years before my release. My two daughters had a stranger for a father. Time and distance got in the way and we lost touch. I remember a saying . . . a plane or a train can take you back to the place but not the time.

I had become a stigma to most of my friends, family and associates during the years that I had been in prison, and a pariah since my release.

So now I live quietly with my girlfriend, in country Victoria.

Where you will find me.

Re-adapting in a leisurely way.

Re-orientating in a slow sloth-like manner.

Re-assimilating at no great speed.

I am moving forward and am now studying how to act in a civilised western manner. Which means I have to stop eating with my hands, or washing my bum with water. I suspect that I carry a great many Asian traits, I just have to work out which traits to keep and which traits to discard.

My only wish is that I could do the same with my memories.

Keep the good, discard the bad.

An old Chinaman once told me
That only fools hold tight to regret,
And only heroes have the strength to rebuild.
The choice is yours.

ACKNOWLEDGEMENTS

I would like to thank a number of people who have stuck with me (sometimes like a tick on a mangy dog) and persevered with my idiosyncrasies and eccentricities throughout my years on this planet.

To those who visited me in prison. To my brother Jeffrey Parnell, who wrote to me religiously every month for 11 years (not that I got all of his letters). His and his wife Karen's steadfast loyalty and belief in me, when many others had failed, helped inspire me to write this book. After all, I couldn't let my big brother down. And to my little brother, Shane, who visited me in Bali's Bunglie Mental Asylum.

Thank you also to my sister Rhonda (Blondi) Parnell, for the lettuce and letters. I love you, sister.

To my sister Lynette, who wrote endless letters on my behalf, and who was once my closest sibling, and her deceased husband Ken Mansfield.

To my friend of over 35 years, Lamiciky (Goldie) Pitt, who was a happy face for me to see in Bali when I was first arrested.

And of course to my intrepid cousin John Elliot Smith, whose happy round smiling face brought me the news of my presidential pardon.

To just say thank you would never be enough. I am indebted to you all.

And of course to my Mother – thank you for all the help you gave me.

To the ladies at HarperCollins: Shona Martyn, Alison Urquhart, Gwenda Jarred, Vanessa Radnidge and Sara Wiggins. To you ladies, my most sincere and humble thank you.

To Ryl and Dave Harrison who visited me in Malang Prison and returned to Australia with my manuscripts and put so much time and effort into getting them typed up for me. I not only thank you, but I also love you guys to bits.

I must also thank Brett and Jill Carrathers, who dipped deeply into their pockets to help me when I was financially destitute and who have showed me the true meaning of the word FRIENDSHIP.

To Bruce and Anne Stewart, who helped me so much during their short stay living in Malang.

To Vince Stanton, Vonny Helberg, and Ibu Swan (Mother Swan) and all those Christian people whose hearts I'm sure God has truly touched. I thank you all and I thank you for your prayers. When the Bible says that God works in strange ways . . . it's really not kidding.

To Miss Yani Lim. Without her this book would have been totally impossible. For without her, I would have been buried alive after the Indonesian doctors had pronounced me dead and had sent my body off to the morgue. THANK YOU YANI. Your gentle forgiving ways, your soft voice and smiling eyes are memories I shall carry for eternity. You changed me in many ways.

To Jan Jodill and Adrian Essenberg, who helped to inspire me to keep writing when things got me down.

I thank also my cousin Cheryl Parnell for all her sweat and blistered fingers. If I had been denied her services and skills, this book would not have been finished for another ten years. Her wit and charm are second to none.

Also a BIG THANK YOU to the lads here in Australia who have helped me so very much since my return to Australia. To John Lynch and the crew. To Big Bad Al, the working girls' pal. And Kenny. For all their assistance when I returned.

To my old mate Malcolm Crompton, who was there for me within the first weeks of my return, loading up my anorexic wallet with enough to buy my first western wardrobe in over 11 years.

To my mad Dutchie mate, Christian Van De Bosch, your trust and loyality are as iron and steel.

To Simon Bashford, a big thank you.

Not forgetting my ex-jockey cousin Bradley Parnell, your happy disposition along with the use of your computer was greatly welcomed and appreciated, mate . . . Thanks, Cus. Just polish up on your jockey rot rash jokes, they're totally unacceptable in public . . .

Finally to the lady who helped me knock off the rough edges and polish this whole project up, including the knocking off of some of the rough edges that I as a rough nut still carry. I thank my lady, Debra June Knight, whose letters over the years would always inspire me and give me strength. A strength that was built on the belief that when someone loves you, you will always find a reason to live.

Christopher V.V. Parnell